Yoga
for everyday living

Yoga
for everyday living

Stella Weller

Bounty
BOOKS

An Hachette UK Company
www.hachette.co.uk

This edition published in 2016 by Bounty Books,
a division of Octopus Publishing Group Ltd
Carmelite House
50 Victoria Embankment
London, EC4Y 0DZ
www.octopusbooks.co.uk

Publisher: Samantha Warrington
Design: Leah Germann
Editor: Anna Southgate
In-house editor: Phoebe Morgan

ISBN: 978-0-75373-014-0

A CIP catalogue record for this book is available from the
British Library

Printed and bound in China

10 9 8 7 6 5 4 3 2 1

CONTENTS

USING THIS BOOK

A good guide shows you the way as you explore new terrain, or helps you to rediscover territory with which you may once have been familiar. This book is such a guide, providing direction, encouragement and wise counsel along the path of your yoga journey. It has been designed for you, the busy person, to show you how to integrate this time-honoured system of health promotion and personal growth into your daily life.

Even if you can spare no more than five minutes a day for exercising, you can combine the exercises to create a workout to suit your own special needs. Before you begin, though, check with your doctor and read the information in Chapter One thoroughly, even if yoga is not new to you. It is here that you will learn what yoga is and is not, and what guidelines you should follow for safe, effective practice.

You will learn what yoga comprises and how it works to help you to cope in an increasingly stressful world. You will read about the advantages of practising in the morning and those to expect from evening practice, and you will find out about various places where you can safely do the exercises. You will discover how you can incorporate many of the exercises into your working day in order to reap the cumulative benefits of this superb healthcare system.

THE YOGA PROGRAMME

Chapter Two offers safe, simple, enjoyable warm-up exercises that will wake you up gently and generate energy for the day. You will also learn essential cooling-down techniques. Chapter Three is devoted to travel. Here you will find techniques that you can practise safely even while on the road, to help in coping with stressful traffic situations. Suggestions are also given for incorporating exercises in Chapter Two to help to make travel the pleasant experience it could be, and to avoid the anxiety, circulation problems, and jet lag with which frequent flyers are often familiar.

Staying calm under pressure, combating fatigue and boosting energy and productivity at work are the topics addressed in Chapter Four, which provides simple but effective techniques that you can weave into the fabric of your daily schedule, to

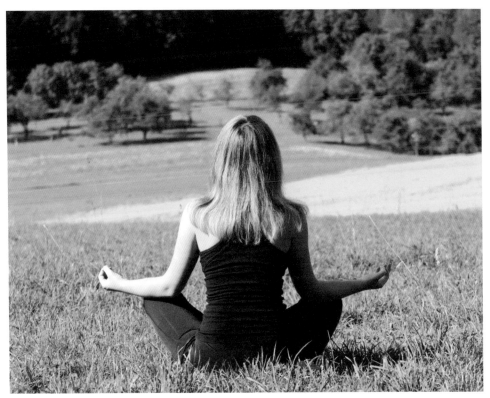

The lack of equipment required means that yoga can be practised anywhere.

help you to act calmly rather than react impulsively. Suggestions are also given for preventing conditions such as backache, neck pain, eyestrain and carpal tunnel syndrome, which prevail in today's fast-moving, highly competitive world.

Returning home after the day's activities often presents another set of challenges. Chapter Five offers a number of 'tools' to help you to unwind and to savour the sanctuary of a warm, secure environment where you can recharge yourself and feel at peace. Among these are breathing techniques that take advantage of one of our most under-utilized natural resources (the breath), and exercises in which you apply the principles of meditation to activities of choice, to induce the state that doctors describe as 'restful alertness'. You will also find out how to promote sound, refreshing sleep without the aid of medication. A specimen yoga programme that you can tailor to suit your unique set of circumstances, is offered for your weekend enjoyment and relaxation.

INTRODUCTION

Because yoga has its roots in the Hindu culture, some people are nervous about practising it. They fear it may be incompatible with their religious beliefs. But this fear is unfounded. Yoga is non-sectarian and may be practised with complete confidence by anyone. If the word itself poses a problem, however, then think of it as a useful package containing safe, simple, effective stress-reduction techniques such as gentle stretching and breathing exercises, and relaxation, concentration and meditation techniques.

THE ASANAS

The physical exercises, called asanas, benefit not only muscles and joints but also internal structures such as organs, nerves and glands. In addition, they train and discipline the mind so as to improve concentration and coordination, and are superb for preventing the build-up of tension that often leads to aches and pains, and that also sometimes causes inappropriate responses and poor impulse control. The exercises are, excellent for improving posture and carriage, thus enhancing self-esteem and self-confidence.

TUNING IN

The mental and breathing exercises (the latter are collectively called pranayama) are probably without match for combating stress, and the relaxation techniques are a very useful adjunct to treatments for disorders such as depression and high blood pressure. Because yoga exercises encourage a full focusing on what is being done, they promote an ability to 'tune in' to yourself, thus fostering the development of a keen sense of awareness which alerts you to the early warning signs of departures from good health. Regular practice will give you a strong sense of balance and wholeness, and of being at peace with yourself.

THE WHOLE PERSON

Yoga differs from many other types of exercise in that it engages the whole person. It requires your full attention during practice, so your mind and body work together to create psychological and physiological harmony.

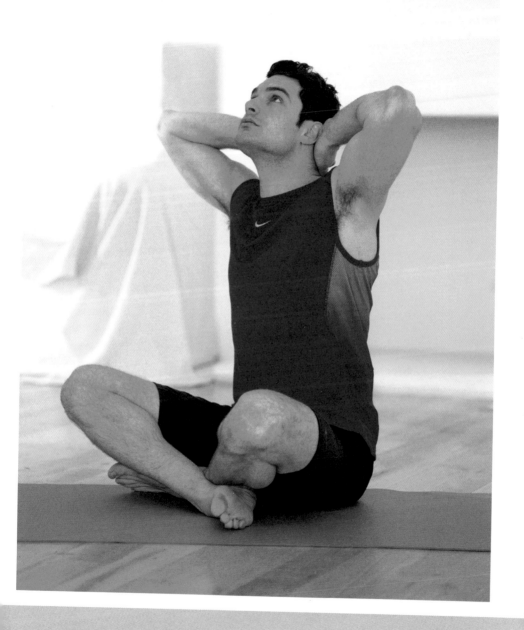

THE BENEFITS OF YOGA

Yoga practice conditions the body and the mind to adapt to environmental influences, both external and internal. Rather than just alleviating symptoms, the exercises address the less evident, but very important, underlying causes of certain states and conditions.

Yoga's stretching, strengthening and meditative exercises are effective because they require full focus on the movements of the body parts involved, in synchronization with attentive respiration (breathing). The mind, discouraged from wandering toward unrelated matters, is kept centred, engendering feelings of being calmer and more organized.

The directing of the attention away from distracting or disturbing stimuli and concentrating it on one thing or activity at a time has a soothing, settling effect. Energy is consequently conserved rather than squandered.

However, yoga is not a 'quick fix'. Do not immediately expect dramatic results. These will be proportionate only to the effort you make. Integrating yoga exercises into activities of daily living, until they become almost second nature, is perhaps the best way of ensuring regularity of practice. In this way, you will not think of them as something to be gotten over and done with, but rather as a pleasurable and anticipated part of day-to-day living.

Through the regular practice of the techniques carried out in this manner, you come to know your body, and you increasingly get in touch with your feelings in a more intimate way than through practising exercises in an automatic, repetitive fashion, which allows the mind to drift randomly. This mindfulness is excellent for promoting calm and control, invaluable attributes for stress-proofing yourself.

Yoga helps to focus the mind.

Practising yoga as a group can help build self-confidence.

CHAPTER 1:
YOGA BASICS

The word yoga comes from Sanskrit, the language of ancient India. It means union, integration or wholeness. It is an approach to health that promotes the harmonious collaboration of the human being's three components: body, mind and spirit.

GETTING STARTED

Perhaps no other period in history has been as fast-paced as the present one. Every day we hurry to fulfil various family and social obligations and to participate in numerous other activities with seemingly unrealistic time constraints. Many people are expected to perform their jobs with the same speed and accuracy as machines. But although machines have become increasingly rapid, humans can work only at a human pace.

HUMAN WEAR AND TEAR

Attempts to accede to the demands of this new technology are made at tremendous cost, both financially and in terms of human suffering. Occupational illnesses such as lower back pain, eyestrain and hand and wrist disabilities are on the rise. The incidence of stress-related disorders such as arthritis, depression and heart disease has increased. But our capacity for dealing with these disorders has not grown proportionately, and mainstream therapies for them do not always have the beneficial effects that we might hope for.

The answer to these problems lies not in exclusive dependence on outside agents such as drugs, but rather in exploring and utilizing our rich store of inner resources.

Rising to the challenge

With the right approach, we can tap into these through the regular practice of yoga, an age-old technology of physical and mental wholeness and personal growth, which requires no props or gadgets, no special clothing or equipment. Yoga now forms the basis of many respected health-promotion programmes and stress-reduction and healing regimens worldwide.

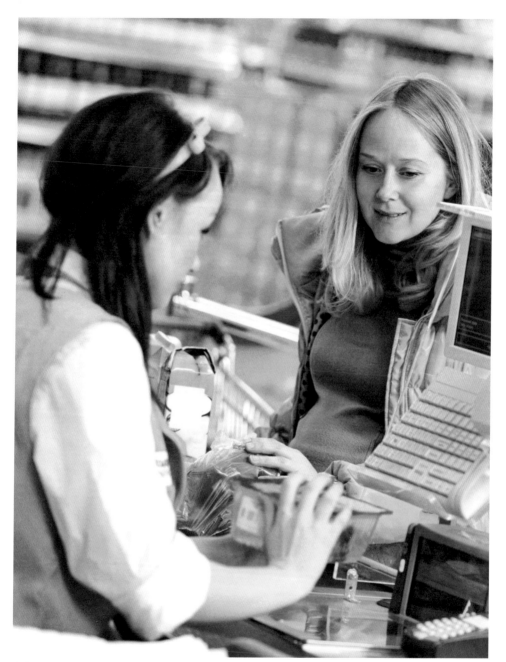

Advances in modern technology have put new strains on day-to-day working life.

INTRODUCING YOGA

Yoga works to maintain health and harmony by encouraging the cultivation of sound psychological attitudes through mental exercises, and breathing and relaxation techniques. It also reconditions the nerve-muscle and nerve-gland systems to enable them to withstand high levels of stress and strain, by means of physical and breathing exercises.

BASIC GUIDELINES

What most characterizes yoga exercises and differentiates them from many other types of exercise is the attentiveness required while doing them. This makes them safe to do because you are promptly alerted to whether you are stretching, bending or turning beyond the point of safety. Before attempting to do any of the exercises, however, check with your doctor. Be especially careful if you have a serious health problem, have had surgery of any kind, or are pregnant.

Before you begin

As a busy person, you will be fitting in the exercises wherever you conveniently can during the course of your day. You are also encouraged to try to set aside a longer period of time each week, for a more

The pose of tranquillity – perfect for combatting stress.

comprehensive yoga session. At such times, start with a few quiet moments to distance yourself mentally from everyday concerns or those that claim your attention at present. Close your eyes. Relax your jaw. Breathe slowly and smoothly. Relax your hands. Set the scene for the exercises you are about to do.

Begin with a few simple warm-ups, such as those offered in Chapter Two. At the end of your exercise session, cool down and recover appropriately. Most of the exercises in Chapter Two, done slowly, are also suitable for this purpose, and many yoga classes end with the pose of tranquillity.

Be sure to wear loose clothing for a session.

Comfort and safety

Remove from your person any object that may cause pressure or injury while practising yoga, such as a tight belt or spectacles. Wear non-constricting clothing to permit ease of movement and breathing. If it is convenient and inconspicuous, loosen your tie or bra and remove your shoes. Emptying your bladder is an added comfort measure, if circumstances allow it.

If preparing for an exercise session of any length (half an hour or more), remember not to exercise within two hours of eating a heavy meal. This caution is particularly important if you have a history of angina (pain in the region of the heart). You may practise one hour after eating a light snack, or you may exercise after

drinking a cup of tea or other non-alcoholic beverage.

If you plan to practise before breakfast, when your blood sugar level is low after a night without food, you may drink a glass of juice or eat something light, such as a slice of wholegrain bread. This is preferable to exercising on an empty stomach.

When to practise

Do appropriate exercises whenever you begin to feel tense, anxious or tired, to prevent these states from reaching a level that is not conducive to calm, productivity and general well-being. Exercising before you start your day's work can counteract morning stiffness and give you energy. Do try a combination of the exercises in Chapter Two whenever possible.

Invest in your own yoga mat to avoid practising on hard floors.

Exercising in the evening can relax you after a challenging day and induce that healthy tiredness that promotes sound, refreshing sleep. You may find a sequence of the exercises described in Chapter Five appropriate. Experiment to determine which times are best for you.

Look for opportunities throughout the day (and if you are a shift worker, during the evening or night) to incorporate appropriate techniques into your schedule. In my clinical practice I have often done this to give relief to tired legs, feet and back.

It is better to exercise for ten minutes every day than for half an hour only once a week. When re-starting after an illness or other interruption, do so gradually and patiently. Avoid trying to make up for lost time.

Where to practise

One of the marvellous things about yoga is that you can practise it in a variety of places, indoors or outdoors, and you can even practise it in places where space is limited. Moreover, you do not need to invest in any manufactured equipment: your body, your breath and your attention are all that you require. Ideally, the place where you practise your exercises should be quiet and well-ventilated. Any distractions should be kept to an absolute minimum. If you are practising at home, ask family members not to disturb you for the duration of your session.

The ground or floor on which you do the asanas should be smooth and level. A carpeted floor is suitable, or you can practise on a non-skid mat. A level grassy surface is also fine. The surface on which you exercise will be referred to as the 'mat' in the exercise instructions throughout this book.

There are many opportunities for incorporating yoga exercises into daily activities. Suggestions are given alongside the instructions for many of the exercises. With practice,

you will quickly build up your own repertoire of what to do.

How to practise

Practise each exercise slowly and mindfully, that is, with full attention to your movements. Synchronize these movements with slow, regular breathing through your nose (unless instructed otherwise), so that the inhaled air is warmed, moistened and filtered before it reaches your lungs. When you have completed a posture, hold it for a few seconds (increasing the duration as you become more practised and have the time), before resuming your starting position. Do not hold your breath during this

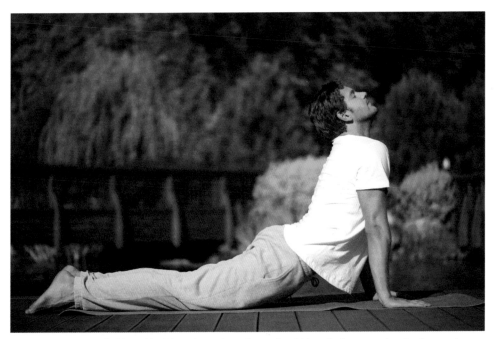

Keep movements fluid and hold each posture for a short time before moving to the next.

pause, which will be referred to as 'hold' in the exercise instructions. Continue to breathe evenly and regularly throughout.

After doing each exercise, take a brief rest. This relaxation period is an important component of muscle activity. It prevents stiffness and the build-up of fatigue.

All movements (unless otherwise stated) should be slow and gentle. Always be on the alert for any sign of resistance or hint of pain in your body. Never attempt to force a movement. Whenever possible, integrate imagery into the exercises to enhance their effectiveness. Try to visualize, for example, the release of tension; blood flowing unobstructed through your body; a lessening of fatigue; feelings of warmth and comfort. Suggestions will be given from time to time with the exercise instructions.

Many postures are fine during pregnancy.

GENERAL CAUTIONS

• Before starting this or any other exercise regime or programme, you should always check with your GP and obtain permission to do so.

• If you suffer from an ear or eye disorder, such as a detached retina, omit any practice of inverted postures such as the half and full shoulderstand (see pp. 128–131) and the dog stretch, which is part of the Sun salutations in Chapter Two (see pp. 43–7).

• Avoid rapid abdominal breathing, as in the dynamic cleansing breath (see pp. 48–9) if you have epilepsy.

• Avoid inverted postures and rapid abdominal breathing if you have high blood pressure or heart disease.

• Always omit practice of the inverted postures during your menstrual period.

• If you have a hernia, you should omit the cobra, which is part of the Sun salutations in Chapter Two.

• Check with your doctor before practising the Sun salutations if you have varicose veins or venous blood clots.

• Pregnant women who have a history of miscarriage are cautioned not to do the exercises in the first three or four months of pregnancy. If the pregnancy is progressing normally, try the warm-ups in Chapter Two, omitting the lying twist (see pp. 36–7, the rock-and-roll (see pp. 40–1) and the Sun salutations (see pp. 43–7). Check with your doctor.

• Postures not recommended during pregnancy include those done lying on the abdomen, as in the cobra. Avoid lying flat on your back after the first trimester (three months), since this can restrict the blood and oxygen flow to mother and foetus, by putting pressure on the inferior vena cava (the principal vein draining the lower part of the body). Avoid squatting after the 34th week of pregnancy, until your baby's head is fully engaged.

'Yoga teaches us to cure what need not be endured and endure what cannot be cured.'

B K S Iyengar

CHAPTER 2:
PREPARING
FOR THE DAY

The first few minutes after waking up can set the pace and tone for the rest of the day. Tumbling out of bed, stumbling to the bathroom, gulping a cup of coffee and dashing out of the house will start you off on a frenetic note. Heavy traffic will ensure that you arrive at school or work feeling under pressure. This chapter will help you to start your day calmly.

WARMING UP

Warm-up exercises help to reduce the bodily stiffness that often occurs after spending many hours in bed. They raise body temperature slightly, improve blood circulation and wake you up gently. They also improve the flexibility and range of motion of the body's joints.

YOGA ON WAKING

Even before you get out of bed, you can make the transition from being asleep to waking up smoother and less jarring to the nerves than bolting out of bed. On waking, lie still and turn your attention to your breathing. Make it progressively deeper. Do about five sets of wrist rotations (see p. 35) and ankle rotations (see p. 42). Stretch from head to feet while inhaling, and release the stretch while exhaling. Sit near the edge of your bed for a minute or so of quiet reflection.

The warm-ups in this chapter are ideal for people with busy lifestyles as they can be integrated into the most hectic of schedules to prevent a build-up of tension. When tension is allowed to accumulate, it often progresses to fatigue, aches, and, not infrequently, to pain, thus detracting from your quality of life and work. Suggestions for finding ways of incorporating the warm-ups into your daily activities are given in the Notes and Suggestions that follow some of the descriptions of the exercises' benefits.

Performing the exercises

Do all the exercises slowly (unless otherwise instructed) and with awareness, synchronizing your movements with regular breathing through your nose. Do not hold your breath at any time.

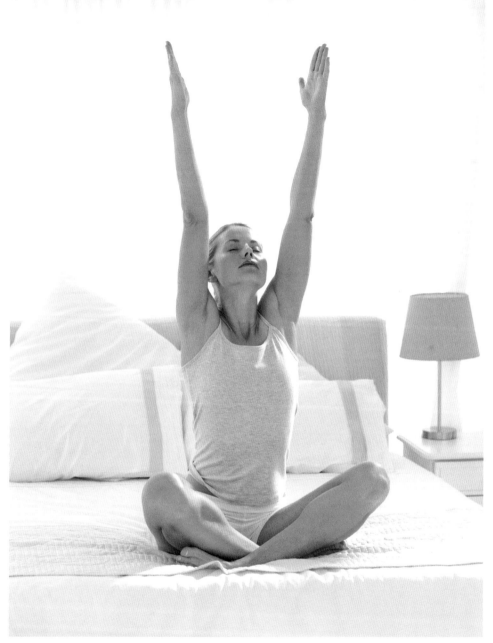

Start your day with a few gentle stretches.

NECK STRETCHES

These stretches are wonderful for helping to keep the cervical (neck) part of the spine flexible and healthy. They also exercise the neck, an area of the body where tension tends to lodge.

NOTES AND SUGGESTIONS

• Many of our daily activities, such as driving a car, sitting at a desk or computer or reading, require a bending forward of the head and the body. This bending can lead to muscle strain, to which the neck is particularly vulnerable.

• To prevent strain, which can and often does progress to aches or pain, it is prudent to take periodic breaks to do compensatory exercises such as the neck stretches. They require you to bring your head upright, crown uppermost and to realign your neck with the rest of your spine. This counteracts the potential ill effects of constantly looking downward. Remember to synchronize your head movements with slow, smooth breathing.

1 Sit or stand comfortably, with the crown of your head uppermost. Fully relax your shoulders, arms and hands.

2 Slowly turn your head as far to the right as you comfortably can.

3 Slowly turn your head as far to the left as you comfortably can.

4 Turn your head to face forward.

5 Support the back of your neck with your hands and slowly tilt your head back to gently stretch the front of your neck.

6 Bring your head upright. Relax your hands and arms.

7 Slowly tilt your chin toward your chest to gently stretch out the back of your neck.

8 Bring your head upright.

9 Repeat steps 2 to 8 several times in succession.

10 Breathe regularly as you complete the exercise. Rest.

Step 2

Step 3

Step 5

Step 7

EAR TO SHOULDER

The benefits of this warm-up are similar to those brought about by the neck stretches (see pp. 28–29). It also exercises the platysma, a broad, flat layer of muscle that extends from each side of the neck to the jaw, so helping to maintain the contour of the neck and improving circulation to the face.

NOTES AND SUGGESTIONS

• Practise the ear-to-shoulder whenever you can throughout the day, especially if you spend much of your time sitting at a desk or a computer, do a great deal of paperwork or reading, or engage in work that requires you to look down or bend forward frequently.

• Practise the exercise during television advertising breaks, while waiting for the kettle to boil or during tea and coffee breaks at your place of work. Look for opportunities to do this and other neck exercises. You may be surprised at how many there are, and you will be pleased to discover what relief such a seemingly simple exercise can bring.

1 Sit or stand comfortably. Keep your shoulders, arms and hands relaxed. Relax your jaw and breathe regularly throughout the exercise.

2 Tilt your head sideways, aiming your right ear to your right shoulder.

3 Bring your head upright.

4 Tilt your head sideways, aiming your left ear to your left shoulder.

5 Bring your head upright.

6 Repeat steps 2 to 5 several times.

7 Rest.

Step 2

Step 4

SHOULDER SHRUGS

The shoulders and upper back are other favourite areas for a great deal of tension to lodge. Shoulder warm-ups discourage tension build-up in the body and enhance the effects of neck exercises. They counteract the fatigue that often results from activities that require much forward bending, and they contribute to improved posture.

NOTES AND SUGGESTIONS

• This simple exercise, practised frequently throughout the day, will do much to prevent the tiredness and tension that often result from spending many hours at a desk, computer, or cash register or, indeed, from any job or activity that generates stress.

Step 2

1 Sit or stand comfortably upright, with the crown of your head uppermost. Relax your arms and hands. Relax your jaw and breathe regularly.

2 Pull your shoulders upward, as if trying to touch both of your ears with them.

3 Hold the shrug for a few seconds, but do not hold your breath.

4 Relax your shoulders.

5 Repeat steps 2 to 4 several times in succession.

6 Rest.

SHOULDER ROTATION

The benefits of this warm-up are the same as those produced by the shoulder shrugs (see p. 32). In addition, shoulder rotation keeps the shoulder joints freely moving and so enhances range of motion and counteracts stiffness. It also conditions the accessory breathing muscles, which help the main respiratory muscles during strenuous exercise and difficult breathing.

NOTES AND SUGGESTIONS

- See the previous exercise (shoulder shrugs) for ideas on when to practise shoulder rotation.

- When taking a warm shower, turn your back to the spray and practise shoulder rotation. It feels wonderful!

1 Sit or stand comfortably upright, with the crown of your head uppermost. Relax your arms and hands. Relax your jaw, also, and breathe regularly.

2 Rotate your shoulders several times in a backward-forward, backward-forward motion.

3 Rest.

4 Repeat the exercise several times.

5 Rest.

Step 2

THE FLOWER

Excellent for improving blood circulation in your hands, the flower also helps to keep your wrists and fingers supple. It prevents tension from building up to the point where it causes pressure on the nerves with resulting pain.

NOTES AND SUGGESTIONS

- When you spend many hours working at a keyboard or cash register, the tendons that move your fingers can swell and exert pressure on the median nerve that runs through the wrist and controls much of the movement, feeling and strength of the hand. This can result in soreness, tenderness and weakness of the thumb muscles, and to numbness and weakness of the fingers. Such symptoms are characteristic of a condition known as carpal tunnel syndrome (CTS).

1 Sit or stand comfortably upright, with the crown of your head uppermost. Relax your shoulders. Relax your jaw and breathe regularly.

2 Hold your hands, made into tight fists, in front of you.

3 Slowly, with resistance, open your hands.

4 Spread out your fingers, and stretch them fully.

5 As a follow-through, stretch your arms sideways and hold the stretch for a few seconds while continuing to breathe regularly.

6 Relax your arms and hands.

7 Finish the exercise by shaking your hands vigorously.

8 Rest.

Step 3

WRIST ROTATION

The benefits of regularly rotating your wrists are the same as those derived from practising the flower exercise (see p. 34).

NOTES AND SUGGESTIONS

• Look for opportunities throughout the day to do wrist rotation and other hand and finger exercises. You may do them, for example, during television advertising breaks or between chores. I do six to eight wrist rotations in each direction before getting up in the morning. This simple procedure has kept my hands pain-free and fully functional over the many years, despite the fact that I have done a great deal of writing and typing.

1 Sit or stand comfortably upright. Relax your shoulders. Relax your jaw and breathe regularly.

2 Rotate your wrists several times in slow, smooth succession, as if drawing circles in the air with your hands: move your left hand clockwise and your right hand counterclockwise.

3 Rest your hands briefly.

4 Repeat the exercise several times in the opposite direction.

5 You may complete the exercise by shaking your hands vigorously a few times, as though trying to rid them of water.

Step 2

THE LYING TWIST

This is an exercise in gentle torsion (twisting), which is necessary for a healthy back. It is also of benefit in toning the abdominal muscles, the condition of which affects the health of the spine.

NOTES AND SUGGESTIONS

- The lower back (lumbar area), between the chest and the pelvis, is one of the structural weak points of the human spine. You can do much to ease back fatigue and to prevent backache by regularly doing strengthening and tension-relieving exercises such as the lying twist or its variation.

- You may want to try doing it in bed (not a waterbed) before getting up in the morning, to counteract any stiffness that may have occurred overnight.

- Consider doing it on a carpeted floor when you come home from work, before doing your evening tasks, to remove residual kinks in your back after a day on your feet or sitting on a chair.

1 Lie on your back, with your arms sideways at shoulder level. Relax your jaw and breathe regularly.

2 Bend your legs, one at a time, and bring your knees towards your chest.

3 Keeping your shoulders and arms in firm contact with the surface on which you are lying, slowly, gently and smoothly tilt your knees to one side as you exhale. You may keep your head still or turn it to the side opposite the tilted knees.

Step 2

4 Inhale and bring your knees back to the centre.

5 Exhale and tilt your knees to the opposite side, keeping your head still or turning it to face opposite the tilted knees.

6 Repeat the side-to-side tilting of your knees (steps 3 to 5) several times in slow, smooth succession.

Step 3

7 Bring your knees to the centre again. Stretch out your legs, one at a time. Relax your arms and hands.

8 Rest.

VARIATION

In the variation of the lying twist you prop yourself on your elbows rather than lying on your back.

1 Start in a sitting position, with your legs stretched out in front of you.

2 Lean back and prop yourself on your elbows.

3 Bend your legs, one at a time, and bring your knees towards your chest.

4 Tilt your knees to one side as you exhale.

5 Inhale and bring your knees back to the centre.

6 Exhale and tilt your knees to the opposite side.

7 Repeat steps 4 to 6 several times in slow, smooth succession.

8 Bring your knees to the centre. Stretch out your legs, one at a time. Relax your arms and hands.

9 Rest.

THE BUTTERFLY

The butterfly exercise helps to reduce stiffness and promote flexibility in the ankle, knee and hip joints. It gently stretches the adductor muscles that run along the inside of the thighs. It also improves circulation to the lower pelvis and the legs.

NOTES AND SUGGESTIONS

- This is excellent for women's reproductive health. You can do as many as 60 repetitions per minute while watching television or waiting for a kettle to boil.

Step 1

1 Sit upright with your legs folded inward, and the soles of your feet together. Clasp your hands around your feet and bring them comfortably close to your body.

2 Alternately lower your knees and raise them, like a butterfly flapping its wings. Do so as many times as you wish, at a slow to moderate pace.

3 Relax your arms and hands, and stretch out your legs, one at a time.

4 Rest.

Step 2

VARIATION

1 Sit with your legs folded inward and the soles of your feet together. Pull your feet a comfortable distance from your body.

2 Support yourself by putting your hands flat on the mat beside you.

3 Alternately lower and raise your knees, as many times as you wish, at a slow to moderate pace.

4 Relax your arms and hands. Stretch out your legs, one at a time.

5 Rest.

Step 2

Step 3

ROCK-AND-ROLL

This is an excellent warm-up that conditions the back and the abdominal muscles. It also exercises the hamstring muscles at the back of the legs, which tend to stiffen and shorten when you spend a lot of time sitting. (The hamstrings affect the tilt of the pelvis, and so have a bearing on posture, as well as on the health of the back.) In addition, when you do the rock-and-roll, you press on 64 traditional acupressure points, all with general health benefits.

NOTES AND SUGGESTIONS

• The rock-and-roll is a good all-over morning warm-up to generate alertness and energy for the day's work. It takes only a minute or two to do between 10 and 20 repetitions. Choose a pace with which you feel completely comfortable.

• Another superb all-body warm-up is the Sun salutation series which follows (see pp. 43–7).

1 Sit on a mat with your legs stretched out in front of you.

2 Bend your legs and place the soles of your feet flat on the mat, close to your buttocks.

3 Pass your arms under your bent knees and hug your thighs. Tuck your head down and your chin in, making your back as rounded as you comfortably can. Relax your jaw and breathe regularly.

4 Inhale and kick your legs back to help you roll on to your back.

5 Exhale and rock forward into a sitting position again. Do not land heavily on your feet as the impact will jar your spine.

6 Repeat the rock-and-roll movements as many times as you wish in smooth succession.

7 Sit or lie down and rest.

Step 1

Step 3

Step 4

ANKLE ROTATION

Rotating your ankles is an excellent way of improving the circulation in your feet and legs, and of increasing flexibility in the ankle joints.

NOTES AND SUGGESTIONS

• Circulation in the feet and legs tends to slow down when we sit a great deal, and the feet may become cold.

• Rotating the ankles during periodic breaks is one way to help maintain good circulation in the legs and feet.

• You can do this simple yet effective exercise in the office, at rest areas along the way during a long trip by car or bus, or watching television.

• You can do it as soon as you wake up in the morning, while sitting near the edge of the bed, feet dangling.

1 Sit where you can move your feet freely. Relax your jaw and breathe regularly through the exercise.

2 Make imaginary circles in the air with your feet: rotate the left ankle clockwise and the right ankle anticlockwise.

3 Repeat step 2 in the opposite direction, several times in slow, smooth succession: rotate the left ankle anticlockwise and the right ankle clockwise.

4 Relax your feet and legs.

Step 2

THE SUN SALUTATIONS

Many of us spend several hours each day sitting at a desk, behind the wheel of a motor vehicle or in front of a television set. Many others of us are on our feet for countless hours, either walking from place to place or standing at a counter, for example.

Such activities or inactivity put us at risk of becoming inflexible. Our joints stiffen from disuse and our muscles atrophy (waste away) to some extent from failure to receive normal exercise. An inflexible body is less efficient and more vulnerable to aches, pains and injury than a flexible one. It is also unlikely to be as trim and energetic. Keeping flexible promotes fitness, energy, stamina and resilience. It contributes to productivity and to the confidence that comes from feeling positive about yourself.

The Sun salutations, consisting of 12 movements, promote the flexibility of the whole body. Each flows gracefully into the next, exercising the spine backward and forward, and stretching and toning the legs. They are done in synchronization with regular breathing and with total awareness.

Some of the movements, such as the cobra (step 7, p.45), can be practised as individual asanas (postures or exercises). Or the entire Sun salutation series can be used as the basis for a mini-workout of your own devising by adding a sideways-bending exercise and/or a spinal twist, so that all four sets of the muscles that form the "abdominal corset" and the complementary spinal muscles may be exercised to some extent during the same yoga practice session.

CAUTIONS

- If you have varicose veins or venous blood clots please check with your doctor before attempting to practise the Sun salutations.

- Please also review the section on general cautions in Chapter One (see p. 21).

1 Stand tall, with the palms of your hands together in front of you as if in prayer. Relax your jaw and breathe regularly.

2 Inhale, stretch your arms overhead, and carefully bend backward. Tighten your buttock muscles to protect your back.

3 Exhale and bend forward, at your hip joints rather than at your waist, and place your hands on the mat beside your feet. Bend your knees, if necessary. As you gain flexibility, you will be able to keep your legs straight.

Step 1

Step 2

Step 3

Step 4

Step 6

Step 5

Step 7

4 Inhale and look up. Taking the weight of your body on both hands, step back with your right foot, keeping your toes pointing firmly forward.

5 Neither inhaling nor exhaling, step back with your left foot. Your body weight is now borne by your hands and feet and is in a straight line from the back of your head to your heels.

6 Exhale and lower your knees to the mat. Also lower your chin (or forehead) and chest to the mat. This is the 'knee-chest' or 'eight points' position.

7 Inhaling, relax your feet so that your toes point backward. Lower your body to the mat and arch your back slowly and carefully. Keep your head up and your hands and hips in contact with the mat. This is the cobra posture.

8 Exhale and point your toes forward, pushing against the mat with your hands to help you raise your hips. Keep your arms as straight as you can and hang your head down. Aim your heels toward the mat but do not strain your hamstring muscles. This is the dog stretch posture.

9 Inhaling, look up, rock forward on to your toes and step between your hands with your right foot.

Step 8

10 Exhaling, step between your hands with your left foot and bend forward.

11 Inhaling, come up carefully into a standing position, and move smoothly into a backward bend, with your arms overhead.

Step 9

12 Exhale and resume your starting position. Repeat all 12 movements, as many times as you wish, alternating the leading leg (see steps 4 and 9) each time.

13 Rest.

Step 10

Step 11

COOLING DOWN

After any exercise session it is important to cool down. This provides a chance for static muscle stretching, which enhances flexibility. It allows your cardiovascular system (heart and blood vessels) to return gradually to normal functioning. It helps to prevent a sudden drop in blood pressure and, in addition, it permits metabolic waste products to be removed from the body, and energy reserves to be replenished.

All the exercises in this chapter, except the rock-and-roll, may be done as cooling-down exercises. Observe good posture when doing them and practise slowly. You may finish your session with a top-to-toe relaxation such as the pose of tranquillity described in Chapter Five (see pp. 132–7).

Step 12

DYNAMIC CLEANSING

A good way in which to help yourself to wake up after a night's sleep is to practise this invigorating breathing exercise. It is also known as the 'bellows' breath', the 'runner's breath' and the 'breath of fire', all of which give some indication of its powerful effects. It takes only about 30 seconds to do 30 of these respirations.

WHAT IT DOES

Wonderful for cleansing the sinuses and other respiratory passages, the dynamic cleansing breath also strengthens the diaphragm, a dome-shaped muscle that separates the chest and abdominal area.

It gives a therapeutic massage to the abdominal organs and provides relief for those who suffer from breathing difficulties such as asthma. The dynamic cleansing breath is also an excellent technique to practise whenever your energy levels drop too low.

NOTES AND SUGGESTIONS

• The abdominal action and the sound of the breath when this exercise is performed are reminiscent of the expanding and collapsing of a bellows as it drives a blast of air into a fire. Visualizing this may help to grasp and master the technique.

• Practise the exercise outdoors whenever you can, provided the air is relatively unpolluted.

• You may practise the dynamic cleansing breath while lying down.

The dynamic cleansing breath is completely different from hyperventilation (overbreathing): it is done consciously and purposefully, whereas hyperventilation is involuntary. The exercise results in thorough exhalation and, consequently, a full, spontaneous inhalation. In hyperventilation, carbon dioxide stores are quickly depleted, with unpleasant effects that include feelings of light-headedness and anxiety. This does not occur during the practice of the dynamic cleansing breath.

1 Sit or stand comfortably. Relax your shoulders, arms and hands. Close your eyes or keep them open, as you prefer. Relax your jaw and breathe regularly.

2 Inhale slowly, smoothly and as fully as you can without strain.

3 Exhale briskly through your nose as if sneezing; focus your attention on your abdomen, which will tighten and flatten.

4 Inhalation will follow naturally as you relax your abdomen and chest.

5 Repeat steps 3 and 4 in rapid succession. Try to do so about six times to start with. Gradually increase the number of repetitions as your stamina improves and you become more familiar with the technique.

6 Resume regular breathing.

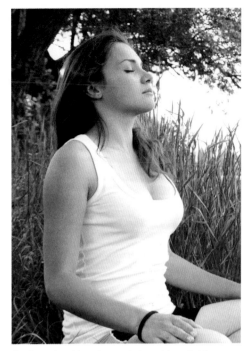

Performing the dynamic breath outside.

CAUTIONS

- Do not practise the dynamic cleansing breath if you suffer from any of the following: high blood pressure, epilepsy, hernia, an ear or eye disorder, or a herniated ('slipped') disc.

- Do not practise it during menstruation or pregnancy.

- Wait for at least two or three hours after eating to practise this exercise.

PREPARING FOR THE DAY

'Yoga cultivates
the ways of
maintaining
a balanced
attitude in
day-to-day life
and endows
skill in the
performance of
one's actions.'

B K S Iyengar

CHAPTER 3:
YOGA FOR TRAVEL

Travelling is an inescapable part of life today.
It can range from a daily commute to and from
the workplace, to short trips for shopping
and business, to family travel for holidays and
reunions. And for increasing numbers
of people, travel involves plane journeys,
some of which last many hours.

BALANCE AND HARMONY

What used to be a relatively low-stress and essentially pleasant activity has now become, for many of us, one that is fraught with apprehension, anxiety and frustration. Population growth, more money, and more accessible air travel are only some of the contributory factors.

URBAN LIFE

City streets are now more congested than ever, traffic during peak hours is painfully slow, and aircraft cabins are generally less spacious, with a recycled air supply. But this gloomy picture is not without relief, and you can do much to find this relief by using your own built-in resources of body, mind and breath.

Apart from travel by public transport, driving to work is perhaps the most common method of transport. It is also one of the most stressful. Before installing yourself behind the wheel in the morning, be sure to have an adequate breakfast as this will contribute to the alertness and evenness of temper you will need to cope with slow-moving traffic or with the lack of consideration shown by some of your fellow motorists.

Breathe for relief

Four breathing techniques that you can practise en route are described in this chapter. Key points to remember when doing them are: maintaining good posture, with the crown of your head uppermost; relaxing your body as much as you can, paying particular attention to your lips, jaw and tongue; breathing in and out through your nose (unless instructed otherwise), and keeping your breathing rhythm slow and even.

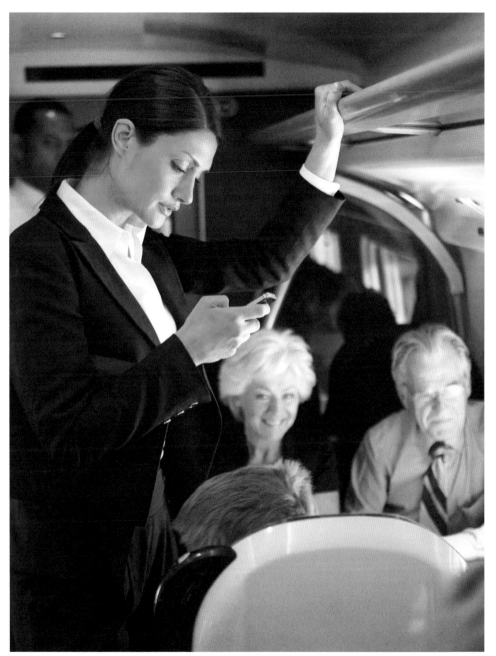

Commuters increasingly find inner-city transport oversubscribed.

ANTI-ANXIETY BREATH

Although the link between respiration and physical states may be readily apparent, the connection between breathing and mental states, while perhaps not immediately obvious, is nevertheless undeniable. Changes in feelings, particularly if they are intense, are reflected in patterns of breathing and can profoundly affect the smooth, continuous flow of breath. But since the relationship between breath and mind is reciprocal, you can bring about a change in emotional climate by consciously altering your breathing pattern.

WHAT IT DOES

This is an excellent exercise to practise before you drive and whenever you are apprehensive or worried. It will help you to maintain control over your actions.

1 Make sure that your head is naturally poised, your chin neither too far down nor up. Hold your steering wheel securely but in a relaxed manner. Make sure that your seat is adjusted so that your legs can reach the pedals without being locked straight. Relax your knees. Sit as far back in your seat as you comfortably can. Relax your shoulders and your jaw and breathe regularly.

2 Inhale quietly through your nose, slowly, smoothly and as completely as you can without any force.

3 Exhale through your nose, slowly, smoothly and as thoroughly as you can without strain.

4 To avoid hyperventilating, count: 'one thousand, two thousand' before inhaling again.

5 Repeat steps 2 to 4 in smooth succession, until your breathing rate is slower and you feel calmer.

6 Resume regular breathing.

Slow-moving traffic raises stress levels.

SIGHING BREATH

This is a wonderful technique for releasing pent-up emotion and for managing stress. Practise it whenever you sense tension mounting or whenever you feel anxious or frustrated. Do not feel self-conscious about practising this exercise while sitting in a tailback or a layby. People will think you are whistling.

NOTES AND SUGGESTIONS

- The sighing breath is also known as 'pursed-lip breathing'.

- It helps to prolong your exhalation and so promotes a sense of control over your respiration, a process that is both involuntary and voluntary.

- It is useful in combating difficult breathing (dyspnoea) and the sense of panic that can accompany it.

1 Check your posture (see step 1 of the anti-anxiety breath, p. 56). Relax your jaw and breathe regularly.

2 Inhale slowly, smoothly, and as deeply as you comfortably can through your nostrils.

3 Exhale steadily through pouted lips, as if whistling or cooling a hot drink (see below). Close your mouth at the end of the exhalation, but do not tighten your jaw or compress your lips.

4 Repeat steps 2 and 3 in smooth succession, as many times as you wish.

5 Resume regular breathing.

Step 3

SNIFFING BREATH

When your chest is so tight that you are unable to take a comfortably deep inward breath, the sniffing breath is the exercise that you should do. It is a wonderful antidote to the build-up of tension in the chest and elsewhere in the body.

NOTES AND SUGGESTIONS

Step 3

- Practising the sniffing breath whenever you feel anxious, upset, or under pressure, will help you stay relaxed and in control.

1 Establish and maintain good posture. Relax your jaw and breathe regularly.

2 Take two, three or more small, quick inward breaths, as if you were breaking up your inhalation into small equal parts.

3 Exhale slowly and steadily through pursed lips.

4 Repeat steps 2 and 3 again, until you feel your chest relaxing and you can take one deep inward breath without straining.

5 Resume regular breathing.

UJJAYI PRANAYAMA

The Sanskrit word *ujjayi* means 'control or victory through expansion'.
Pranayama is the word used to describe yoga's breathing exercises.
Ujjayi pranayama is sometimes referred to as 'breath with sound' or 'the victorious breath'.

WHAT IT DOES

This breathing exercise improves the ventilation of the lungs, calms frayed nerves and replenishes energy.
It helps to slow down the heartbeat and so ease the heart's workload.
It also contributes to a strengthening of the immune system, which protects the body from invasion by harmful organisms.

As an introduction to this technique, imagine that you're blowing on to a windowpane to make it foggy by whispering the syllable 'haa' (see right). This will help you to bring about the relaxation of your throat that is necessary for the execution of the breathing exercise itself.

Now you're ready to begin.

1 Relax your jaw, keeping your lips closed though not compressed. Inhale slowly through your nose while pretending to say 'haa'.

2 Exhale slowly and completely through your nose, with your mouth still closed, while again pretending to say 'haa'.

3 Repeat steps 1 and 2 again and again in smooth succession. Listen for a regular, smooth sound, which will indicate a sense of calm, in contrast with a rough, uneven sound, which suggests some agitation.

4 Resume regular breathing.

Preparing for the exercise

LONGER ROAD JOURNEYS

The demands of a long road journey can tax the driver's resources to the limit and put a strain on the interpersonal relationships of the vehicle's occupants. The key to avoiding this is to forestall the build-up of tension, which can be insidious. By practising simple exercises en route and also at rest stops along the way, there is a good chance that you can expect to arrive at your destination with energy to spare, rather than exhausted and bad-tempered.

When you arrive at your destination, you will benefit from taking a few moments to rest your eyes and, indeed, your whole body and your mind. Sit somewhere comfortable or lie down, close your eyes, and practise any of the breathing exercises described in this chapter. For a top-to-toe relaxation, practise the pose of tranquillity, described in Chapter Five (see pp. 132–7; and see also below).

EVERY LITTLE HELPS

Although the exercises you will be incorporating each day into your activities are simple and take very little time, do not think that they are insignificant. Their effects are cumulative and you will begin to notice the benefits in time. What really matters is the regularity with which you integrate the exercises into your daily life.

The pose of tranquillity

EYES: PALMING

Drivers expend a great deal of energy through their eyes. After hours of defensive driving, the eyes can become very strained. Park your vehicle safely and practise the following exercise to counteract eyestrain, prevent tension build-up in your face and body, and promote concentration.

1 Sit where you can rest your elbows: on a picnic table or even on the steering wheel of your parked car.

2 Rub your palms together vigorously to warm them up.

3 Rest your palms gently over your closed eyes to shut out the light. Do not put pressure on your eyeballs. Relax your jaw. Breathe regularly.

Step 3

4 Stay in this position for a minute or two. If you wish, you may keep your eyes closed but again rub your palms together and continue the palming for a further minute or two.

5 Separate your fingers so that the light is slowly reintroduced. Relax your arms and hands.

6 To finish the exercise, blink several times to lubricate your eyes with natural moisture.

Step 5

GENTLE STRETCHES

Any journey involves sitting or standing in the same position for a given length of time. When travelling long distances, this can be for hours. People often say they need to stretch their legs on arrival somewhere and this it true for all limbs – they need to recover from repeatedly being held in the same position and the best way to do this it to stretch.

THE NECK

With your vehicle safely parked, sit on a log, bench, or boulder and with your eyes either closed or open, practise neck stretches (see right and below; pp. 28–9) and the ear-to-shoulder exercise (see pp. 30–31).

THE SHOULDERS

Sit on a suitable prop, such as a bench or a fallen tree, or even on the grass. You may also stand. Relax your jaw and breathe regularly. Shrug your shoulders (see p. 32) and do shoulder rotations (see p. 33).

You may also try one or both of the exercises for the shoulders and upper back: the chest expander (see p. 80) and the posture clasp (see p. 81), which have the added benefit of improving posture.

Neck stretch to the right

Neck stretch to the left

ARMS AND HANDS

While sitting or standing, practise the flower (see below and also p. 34) and wrist rotation (see p. 35).

FEET AND LEGS

Find a suitable prop on which you can sit and that allows you to move your legs freely. Practise the ankle rotation (see p. 42). You may also alternately bend and straighten your legs to keep the knee joints moving freely and improve your circulation in general.

(see below and also p. 34) and wrist rotation (see p. 35). (see p. 42)

HIDDEN RESOURCES

• Let us not forget the rich, largely untapped store of personal resources we have within us wherever we are: our powers of concentration, our ability to form mental pictures and our breath. Though they are intangible and cost no money, these have the power to transform our lives. With faithful practice, we can become skilled in using these 'tools' to improve our health, our productivity and, indeed, our joy in living.

Flower, step 1

Flower, step 2

THE RAG DOLL

Like any all-over stretch, synchronized with regular breathing, the rag doll will help to counteract bodily stiffness and replenish energy reserves. The rag doll may not be appropriate if you have a history of high blood pressure. Please check with your doctor.

NOTES AND SUGGESTIONS

Step 4

- Try combining imagery with this exercise to enhance its relaxing effects. While dangling, visualize all your accumulated tiredness draining away. You may also do the backward and forward bends in the Sun salutation series (see pp. 43–7), and for a lateral (sideways) stretch you could include the half moon posture (see pp. 146–7).

1 Stand tall. Relax your arms at your sides. Relax your jaw and breathe regularly.

2 Tilt your head forward, bringing your chin toward your chest.

3 Let your shoulders droop and keep your arms and hands limp.

4 Slowly curl your body forward. Let the weight of your arms pull your body down until it hangs loosely. Dangle your arms.

5 Stay in this posture for as long as you wish while breathing regularly.

6 Slowly uncurl your body until you are once again standing upright.

7 Sit or lie down and rest.

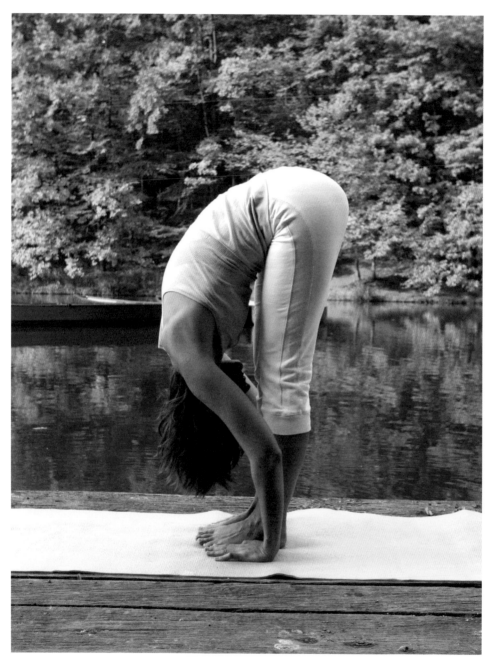

With practice, you will be able to rest your palms flat on the floor.

AIR TRAVEL

Whereas road travel offers opportunities to park at convenient areas along the way to practise certain tension-relieving exercises, air travel does not. Nevertheless, there are many in-flight techniques that you can use to reduce the stress of flying and help to make it a pleasant experience.

AT THE AIRPORT

With the phenomenal increase in air travel in recent years, there has been a higher incidence of flight delays. Waiting at airports can be tedious, and there is only so much reading you can do while waiting to board the plane, before your eyes and your whole body begin to feel fatigued.

Waiting to board a flight

Breathing techniques

Since you may not wish to practise exercises that call attention to yourself, why not use a tool that you carry with you everywhere, your breath? Practise the anti-anxiety breath (see p. 56) and the sniffing breath (see p. 58), both of which can be done unobtrusively. You can do both standing or sitting and without drawing attention to yourself. Or you may wish to try a simple breath meditation, known as breath observation (see p. 68), which will divert your attention from the delay of your flight and its concomitant frustration, and will reduce tension build-up, promoting a sense of calm and control.

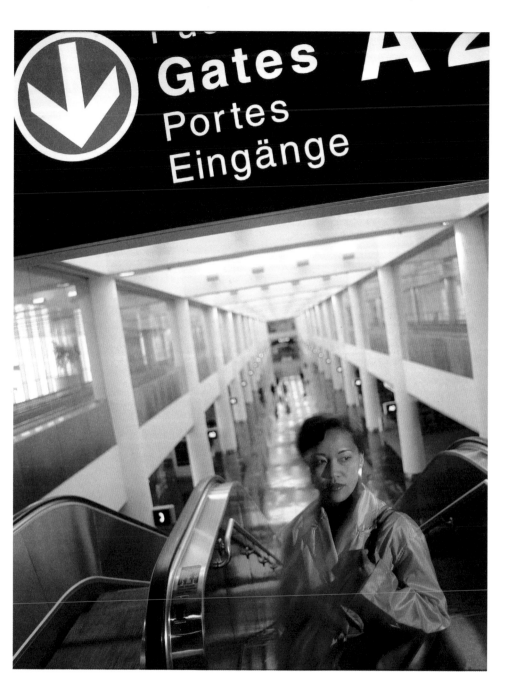

Escalators and travelators provide brief opportunities for practising breathing exercises.

BREATH OBSERVATION

The object of this exercise is to keep your attention on the breathing cycle and to contemplate it. Start with a couple of minutes of practice, and increase the time as you become more familiar and comfortable with it.

NOTES AND SUGGESTIONS

Step 1

• Once in the cabin you may practise any of the breathing exercises referred to in the previous section. Remember to relax your jaw by unclenching your teeth. This has the added advantage of discouraging the facial tension that can lead to headaches.

1 Sit or stand comfortably, with good posture. Relax your shoulders and hands. Relax your jaw and breathe regularly.

2 With your eyes open or closed, focus your attention only on your breathing, without manipulating it in any way. Become a silent observer of your own breathing process: note the rate of breathing, the depth or shallowness of each breath, the smoothness or unevenness, the sounds of quietness or otherwise and the natural pause that occurs between exhalation and inhalation.

RELIEVING TENSION

Flying anywhere often involves sitting in a tight space, with fellow travellers close by. There are few opportunities for getting up and walking about to stretch limbs to relieve them of tension.

SHOULDERS AND UPPER BACK

To prevent an accumulation of tension in your shoulders and upper back, squeeze your shoulder blades together while inhaling and relax them while exhaling. Do this a few times in succession. No one will know what you are doing.

Shoulder rotation

LOWER BACK

Keep the small of your back (waist level) well supported with a small cushion or a rolled-up garment or towel. Practise pelvic tilting, as follows (see also pp. 82–3), to discourage backache and back fatigue. Inhale slowly and smoothly through your nose. As you exhale steadily, press the small of your back toward the back of your chair.

Hold the pressure as long as your exhalation lasts. Inhale and relax your back. Repeat several times. Relax, breathing regularly.

LEGS AND FEET

Unless you are travelling in a cabin with ample space to stretch out your legs, it may be difficult to do exercises to maintain good circulation in the legs and feet, but you can practise ankle rotation (see p. 42).

On a long-haul flight, you can periodically walk to the washroom to relieve tension. Here you can also take the opportunity of doing a few neck stretches (see pp. 28–9) and ear-to-shoulder exercises (see pp. 30–1).

'When the breath wanders, the mind also is unsteady. But when the breath is calmed the mind too will be still... Therefore, one should learn to control the breath.'

Hatha Yoga Pradipika

CHAPTER 4:
YOGA AT WORK

For many of us, the workplace has become a fast-paced, high-pressure environment. Each day we are confronted with such challenges as deadlines, uncertainty about job security and various frustrations that include those connected with our interpersonal relationships. Is it any wonder, then, that we often return home feeling exhausted, drained and discouraged?

YOUR PLACE OF WORK

The number of hours we spend at our place of work each year represents a significant portion of our lives. What a waste it is if work is seen as a necessary evil rather than something satisfying and meaningful. Even if you're not among the remarkably lucky few who love what they do so passionately that they cannot differentiate it from being on vacation, there are simple, effective measures you can take to counteract the stresses inherent in the work environment.

You can practise yoga at work. You can practise it, too, even if you have a home-based business.

BREATHE EASY

Before looking for outside solutions to difficulties that arise from time to time, start first with something you have with you wherever you are: your breath. It is perhaps your most underutilized stress reduction 'tool'. Try this: when next you feel anxious, angry, or frightened, unclench your teeth, keeping your lips together but not compressed. Slow down your rate of breathing. Breathe in and out through your nose but pretend you are breathing through your mouth. You'll be amazed at how quickly this will relax your chest and allow you to breathe more deeply and easily. And because breathing and emotions are very closely linked, you will experience a noticeable lessening of your anxiety, anger or fear.

LEARN TO RELAX

At the same time, relax your hands instead of making them into fists. Form a mental picture in which you see your tension escaping through your hands. Check your facial muscles also, replacing a frown with a relaxed smile.

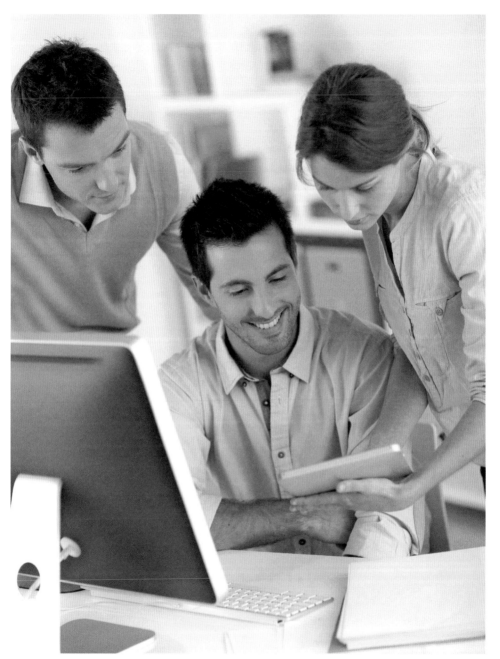

Challenges in the workplace are easier to face if you are calm and relaxed.

EYES

Many of us spend hours each day working at a computer, reading, writing or doing other close work. With the possible addition of glare, our eyes become very vulnerable to eyestrain, which can contribute to headaches or a general feeling of fatigue. Take a short break about once every hour and practise one or two of the following eye exercises, some of which may even be done at your desk.

NOTES AND SUGGESTIONS

Glare is considered the single biggest cause of eyestrain, especially when you use a computer. Here are some suggestions for protecting your eyes.

- Avoid placing your monitor in direct light, sunlight or other light source.

- Fluorescent overhead lights are notorious for causing glare. Consider turning off those directly above your monitor, and perhaps using a small portable light instead.

- Consider also the use of a glare screen, available at computer stores, which can be attached to the front of your monitor.

- Check with your eye specialist about using spectacles for glare prevention, even if you don't need a prescription to correct your sight.

- Avoid staring at the screen for long periods without a break. This tends to produce dryness of the eyes. Periodically, look at a distant object and blink several times, as described in the first two eye exercises.

Eyestrain is a common problem at work.

Exercise your eye muscles while looking in the mirror.

1 Look away from your monitor or other work source every so often. Focus your attention for several seconds, or a minute or more, on a distant object instead. Pay attention to your breathing, checking to see if you are breathing regularly with teeth unclenched and your jaw relaxed.

2 Blink your eyes frequently throughout the day to moisturize them with natural fluid.

3 Put your eye muscles through a range of motion to strengthen and also relax them. With your head still, the crown uppermost and your shoulders relaxed, look to your left, then to your right. Look up, then down. Repeat these four movements several times. Keep your jaw relaxed.

4 Practise palming (see p. 61) to give your eyes relief from light and glare.

SHOULDERS, UPPER BACK AND NECK

Two favourite areas for tension to lodge and accumulate are the shoulders and upper back. Neck pain is frequently reported to doctors. Among its causes are prolonged sitting on chairs or at the wheel of vehicles, poor posture and an unrelieved bending forward of the head. This results in muscle strain and pressure on nerves, which can also contribute to headaches.

THE SHOULDERS AND UPPER BACK

Activities requiring a lot of bending forward tend to promote pain in the shoulders and the upper back, as does habitual poor posture.

Exercises to try

To decrease the incidence of problems related to tension build-up and strain in the shoulders and upper back, practise shoulder shrugs (see p. 32) and shoulder rotation (see p. 33) during short breaks from work. You could also try the chest expander (see p. 80) and the posture clasp (see p. 81) whenever you can.

THE NECK

To compensate for constantly looking downward, to prevent a build-up of tension, fatigue and pain in the neck and adjacent areas and to maintain feelings of comfort, take short periodic breaks from work and practise the neck stretches (see pp. 28–9) and the ear-to-shoulder exercises (see pp. 30–1).

If it is not convenient to do these exercises at your desk, look for a place where you can practise them inconspicuously, such as in a washroom, behind a filing cabinet or even in your car while parked.

Neck stretch, step 3

Neck stretch, step 4

CHEST EXPANDER

This exercise is superb for reducing tension build-up in your shoulders and upper back. It also helps to improve posture and facilitates deep breathing.

NOTES AND SUGGESTIONS

• Practise the chest expander throughout your working day if you spend a great deal of time at a desk or engaged in activities that require you to bend forward.

1 Stand tall, with the crown of your head uppermost and your arms relaxed at your sides. You may also practise this exercise sitting where you can swing your arms freely behind you. Relax your jaw and breathe regularly.

2 Swing your arms behind you and interlace the fingers of one hand with those of the other. Stay upright.

3 Raise your arms upward to their comfortable limit and keep them straight (see right).

4 Hold the raised-arms posture as long as you comfortably can while breathing regularly.

5 Lower and relax your arms and hands.

6 You may finish by shrugging or rotating your shoulders a few times.

7 Rest.

Step 3

POSTURE CLASP

This exercise helps to prevent stiffness in the arm and shoulder joints, keeping them freely moving. It also counteracts the effects of poor postural habits.

NOTES AND SUGGESTIONS

- If you can't interlock your fingers in step 3, use a scarf to extend your arms: toss one end over your shoulder, reaching behind and below to grasp the other end.

1 Sit or stand tall, with the crown of your head uppermost. Relax your jaw and breathe regularly.

2 Reach over your right shoulder with your right hand. Point your elbow upward rather than forward, and keep your arm close to your ear.

3 With your left hand, reach behind your back, from below, and interlock your fingers with those of your right hand.

4 Hold this posture as long as you comfortably can while breathing regularly.

5 Resume your starting position and rest briefly.

6 Repeat the exercise, changing arms, so that your left elbow now points upward (steps 2 to 5).

7 You may finish the exercise by shrugging your shoulders or rotating them a few times.

8 Rest.

Step 3

PELVIC TILT

Lower back pain is widespread, and not only in the workplace. You can greatly decrease your chances of being a sufferer by incorporating a few simple measures into your daily activities. The focus of the pelvic tilt exercise is to help you to keep your back correctly aligned while sitting and standing, thus reducing the likelihood of developing lower back pain in the first place.

NOTES AND SUGGESTIONS

- Practise the sitting pelvic tilt at your desk, during meetings, in the cafeteria or in your parked car.

- Women can use both the sitting and standing version as ante- and postnatal exercises for strengthening the back and the abdomen.

- Practise the standing version of the pelvic tilt several times throughout the day wherever you find a handy prop and can do it unobtrusively. You can try it while in a queue or even during a conversation, if you feel comfortable doing so.

Standing variation

1 Find a suitable prop such as a post, the wall of an elevator or a stable piece of furniture.

2 Stand with your back to your chosen prop and inhale slowly and smoothly through your nose.

3 Exhale and press the small of your back toward the prop. Hold the pressure for the duration of your exhalation.

4 Inhale. Relax your back.

5 Repeat steps 2 to 4 a few more times.

6 Rest.

Standing variation, step 2

Standing variation, step 3

Sitting variation

1 Inhale slowly and smoothly through your nose.

2 On your exhalation, press the small of your back (waist) toward the back of your chair.

3 Hold the pressure as long as your exhalation lasts.

4 Inhale. Relax your back.

5 Repeat steps 2 to 4 a few more times.

6 Rest.

HANDS AND FEET

In order to build a regular yoga routine into your day-to-day life, you need to find time for the discipline at work. Plan to take frequent short breaks during your daily work routine and practice a few short exercises.

HANDS AND ARMS

Review the section on exercises for the hands in Chapter Two. Practise the flower (see p. 24) and wrist rotation (see p. 25). Because the muscles of your wrists are connected to those of your arms, shoulders and neck, remember to do appropriate exercises for those parts also. The chest expander (see p. 80) will give a therapeutic stretch to your arms, and is a good complement to the hand and wrist exercises.

The butterfly

LEGS AND FEET

Stretch out your legs periodically to help maintain good circulation. Whenever you conveniently can, practise ankle rotation (see p. 42). Do not cross your legs while working, as it can constrict blood flow and impair sensation, causing your legs to tingle or 'go to sleep'.

Find opportunities to walk: take the stairs instead of the elevator. Take short walks outdoors, if facilities for this are available, to stretch your leg muscles and give a boost to your circulation. Do breathing exercises of your choice while walking.

Wrist rotation

THE WHOLE BODY

Treat yourself during breaks throughout your working day to a therapeutic all-over stretch: inhale and reach upward with both arms; exhale and lower and relax your arms.

If you wish to stretch sideways, try the half moon (see pp. 146–7) or an appropriate modification. Finish with the rag doll (see pp. 64–5).

MY EXPERIENCE

When I worked in hospital, I would often use my lunch break to replenish my reserves away from the hustle and bustle of the ward. I would go to a quiet spot on the grounds among the trees and flowers and sit in contemplation. Or I would retreat to the small Japanese-style garden surrounded by a bamboo fence and listen to the water trickling over the rocks or admire the foliage or the stone lanterns. Sometimes I would do a simple meditation.

I would return to work feeling more tranquil than when I left, and a worthier resource for those who depended on me. This was in marked contrast with those times when I chose to remain in the cafeteria where the incessant chatter was not conducive to calm and composure.

On night shift, during my main break from work, I often did a lying version of an all-body stretch known as the stick posture, which can also be done while standing. It is a sustained top-to-toe stretch done while lying on the back, with the toes pulled toward the body and the arms overhead. When the stretch was released, I would sink further into the surface on which I was lying with each exhalation. Within ten minutes, I would sense a noticeable lessening of my initial tension and fatigue.

A stretch at your desk promotes relaxation.

BREATH COUNTING

Borrowed from the Zen masters, this apparently simple breathing exercise is extremely effective at calming the body and mind. It temporarily diverts your attention from everyday concerns and disturbing stimuli, and helps you to become more focused and consequently more in control, not only of yourself, but also your life.

NOTES AND SUGGESTIONS

• Do not count higher than four. If you find yourself at seven or eight or higher, you will know that your attention has strayed, and you will need to redirect it and start again at one.

• Give your complete attention to the counting, synchronized with your breathing. When you are aware that your thoughts have strayed to other matters, gently but firmly bring them back to the counting and the breathing.

• Finish your meditation gradually; you should never end abruptly.

1 Sit upright, with the crown of your head uppermost. Close your eyes or keep them open, as you prefer. Relax your jaw and breathe regularly. Let your breath come in and go out naturally, and as you progressively relax, it will become slower and smoother.

2 As you exhale, mentally count 'one'.

3 Inhale.

4 On the following exhalation, mentally count 'two'.

5 Repeat steps 2 and 3 in slow, smooth succession, up to a mental count of four.

6 Repeat steps 2 to 5, as often as you wish.

7 Resume regular breathing without counting.

STRESS REDUCTION

All the exercises in this book encourage self-observation. This helps you to develop a sort of 'tuning in', which will alert you to rising stress levels. You can then promptly take appropriate steps to prevent these levels from rising beyond your control. Here are some tips you can apply at work and elsewhere to help you to cope with everyday stresses.

BE INFORMED

Make the effort to find out about any conditions you might have. The more informed you are about stress, its signs and symptoms, and what it can do to you, the better equipped you will be to cope with it.

KEEP FIT

Attaining and maintaining the best possible level of fitness will give you stamina and resilience for dealing effectively with any difficulties that you encounter. All the asanas (postures or exercises) and breathing,

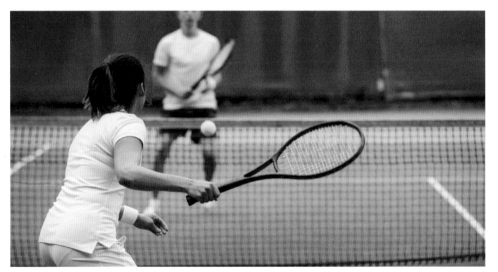

Playing a sport can help to achieve a perfect work/play balance.

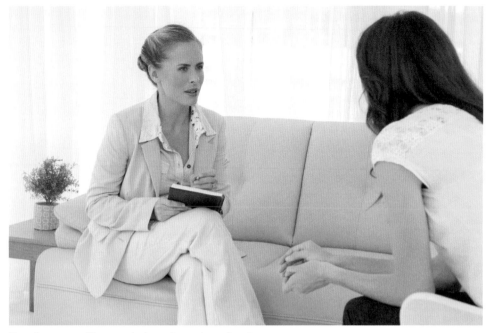

Regular counselling can help reduce stress levels.

relaxation and meditation exercises in this book, practised regularly, will do much to promote optimum wellness.

Incorporating the tension-relieving techniques into daily schedules will help to prevent the build-up of tension that may sometimes cause you to act impulsively, and which also generates fatigue, aches and pains.

EMOTIONAL SUPPORT

It is vital that you establish and preserve a reliable emotional support system consisting of one or more people. This could be a trusted, dependable friend or friends; a professional counsellor with whom you have a good rapport; or a pastor or other spiritual advisor.

SOLID SUPPORT

A solid support system will provide you with inspiration when you feel discouraged, and a healthy outlet for feelings that are better expressed than suppressed. It will, moreover, reinforce positive emotions and promote a sense of self-worth and self-confidence, attributes that are often eroded when you feel dejected and hopeless.

ANGER MANAGEMENT

Learn to channel your anger into constructive outlets, such as exercise. Learn to speak up if you have a problem; to be assertive rather than aggressive. Make enquiries about anger management courses.

SMILE

During the first few seconds of a stressful situation try this: Smile inwardly and with your eyes and mouth. Take a slow, smooth inward breath, as deep as you can without straining. Exhale steadily while letting go of tightness in your jaw, tongue, hands and shoulders. Tell yourself that you are calm, alert and in control.

SIMPLIFY YOUR LIFE

Determine who and what are truly of most value to you and give most of your time and energy to those people and things. Resist the temptation to equate simplicity with deprivation.

SAY NO!

Learn to say 'no'. This is one of the most difficult stress-reduction strategies for many people to put into practice because of the associated feelings of guilt. The ability to say 'no' firmly but graciously prevents the over-commitment that adds to the frustrations of a busy schedule.

PLAY FOR PLEASURE

Experts in the field of mental health agree that play is very important for well-being, which contributes to the ability to cope. Balance your work with a hobby or sport that you are passionate about or greatly enjoy. Avoid bringing a spirit of competition to your recreation.

SELF-ESTEEM

Love and respect yourself. Low self-esteem is a form of self-rejection, which is perhaps the ultimate stressor.

TIME MANAGEMENT

Effective time management is an essential part of stress reduction. But finding enough time for all the things you want or need to do can indeed be very stressful. It can result in a feeling of intense pressure, which sometimes borders on desperation. Once you learn to identify your priorities, devise a plan, and put it into action, you can relieve much of the distress. The key is to 'work smart', rather than longer or harder. Here are some tips to help you to avoid time- wasting:

Reduce clutter
Clutter detracts from effectiveness. Keep your work areas and surroundings organized.

Use your time wisely
Use part of your tea and coffee breaks to reduce tension build-up and replenish energy stores. If you cannot reduce the time you spend commuting to and from work or driving children to and from various activities, then see if you can profit in some way from the travel time. You could listen to an educational cassette while driving, or share the school run with a friend.

Plan your work
Time spent planning what you'll do and when is well invested, as it saves time in the long run. It can avoid having to re-visit a project, which can be stressful.

Be focused
Regularly practise some form of meditation to train you to be more centred and therefore able to concentrate better. Explore any tendencies to delay doing certain tasks – perhaps the most difficult ones –and try to find ways of overcoming this bad habit. Protect yourself from interruptions while you are working. It is the amount of uninterrupted time devoted to a given job that is significant.

Avoid perfectionism
Perfectionism generates frustration, a powerful stressor. Strive instead for excellence of effort and performance.

Work intelligently
Distinguish between those activities that bring positive results and those that you do merely to pass the time.

Delegate chores
Keep your home clean and reasonably tidy but not sterile. Delegate chores to family members and make sure they are done.

Stay well and relax
Failure to take care of your health can result in days off work, which is another major time-waster. Nurture your spirit as well as your body: visit an art gallery, go to a concert or go on a retreat. You will return to your normal activities with renewed enthusiasm, greater productivity and an enhanced sense of accomplishment.

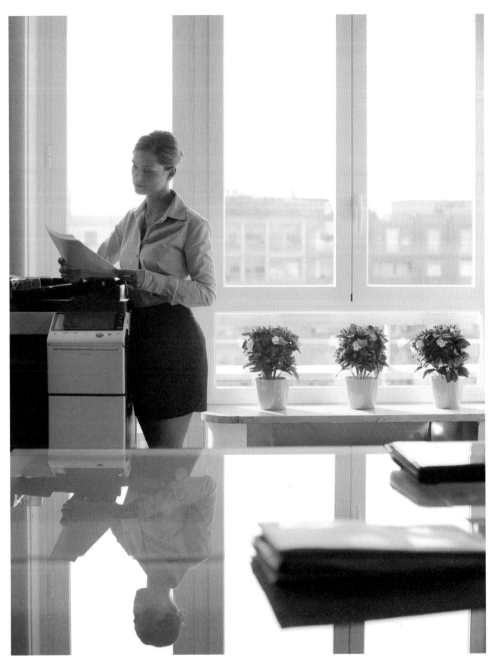

Good organization at work promotes a clear head.

'Yoga does not remove us from the reality or responsibilities of everyday life but rather places our feet firmly and resolutely in the practical ground of experience.'

Donna Farhi

CHAPTER 5:
YOGA AT HOME

Home is a safe haven that offers us shelter and protection from the myriad stresses of the outside world. But that does not mean that it is without other challenges. When you get home from work you may well have chores to do, children to attend to and meals to prepare. Nevertheless, home presents many opportunities for rest and relaxation.

REST AND RELAXATION

On arriving home, try to reserve the first five or ten minutes to help you to adjust from the activities of the workplace and the hum of traffic. This is time very well spent as it can set the tone for the rest of the evening.

You can incorporate a number of yoga techniques into your evening agenda. While waiting for a kettle to boil or a meal to cook, for example, you could do a balancing posture to help strengthen your powers of concentration.

Other exercises you can do while working in the kitchen in the evening include the chest expander (see p. 80) and the posture clasp (see p. 81), which are two of my favourites. You can also practise most of the exercises described in Chapter Two, and you can benefit from the eye exercises in Chapter Four (see pp. 76–7). You may also want to try the meditation in action exercise (see pp. 112–13), which you can modify to suit yourself

WHEN TO MEDITATE

A good time to meditate is before you've eaten your evening meal. The firm posture (see p. 115) and the easy pose (see pp. 116–17) are ideal for meditation at this time.

You can also practise breathing techniques while doing your chores. This is one of the quickest and most effective ways of combating fatigue, restoring energy and promoting calm.

First, do a quick mental head-to-toe check: release any tension in your jaw, lips, shoulders and hands. Next, check your rate of breathing. If it's too fast, slow it down. If it's too shallow, do the sniffing breath (see p. 58) and the sighing breath (see p. 57).

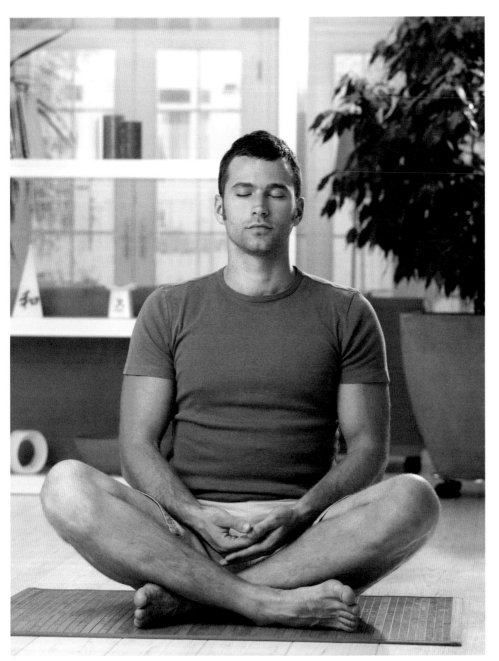

Develop a routine for evening and weekend meditation.

LEGS-UP

The legs-up posture is wonderful for relieving tired, aching legs and feet. By helping the flow of blood from the legs to the heart, and lessening the wear and tear on the valves, it is also excellent for discouraging the formation of varicose veins. Avoid this posture if you have recently-formed blood clots.

NOTES AND SUGGESTIONS

Practise a breathing exercise of your choice or all-body breathing (see p. 99) while in this posture.

1 Lie facing a wall. Lift your legs and rest your feet against the wall, so that they form an angle of about 45 degrees with the surface on which you are lying.

2 Relax your arms, close your eyes and breathe regularly. Stay here for as long as you can (five or ten minutes will suffice).

3 When you are ready, get up slowly and carefully: bring your knees in toward your abdomen, roll on to your left or right side and gently move into a sitting position.

Step 1

ALL-BODY BREATHING

All-body breathing enhances the ability to form pictures in your mind, a process known as visualization or imagery. It is not merely wishful thinking, daydreaming or fantasizing, which are passive and unfocused. Visualization is active and purposeful.

During the past decade or two, researchers have discovered and documented that almost anyone can learn to control functions formerly thought to be entirely involuntary, such as heart rate, blood pressure and blood flow to various parts of the body.

When you visualize certain changes you wish to take place in your body, they tend to occur even though you may be unaware of the underlying mechanisms that bring them about.

1 Lie on your back. Relax your arms at your sides, palms turned upward. Close your eyes. Relax your jaw and breathe regularly.

2 As you inhale, imagine that you are being breathed into, so that you are the unresisting recipient of breath. Visualize your torso enlarging, and every cell absorbing life-giving properties from the air entering your body.

3 With the outflow of air during exhalation, visualize your body gently contracting in size, as various metabolic waste products are expelled from it.

4 Fully focus your attention on the pulsating of your abdomen as it rises and falls.

5 Repeat the exercise (steps 2 to 4) for about ten breath cycles (inhalations and exhalations) at first. You can increase the number of cycles as you become more familiar and comfortable with the visualization, and as time permits. Totally surrender yourself to the surface on which you are lying, and observe the process as if you were a silent witness looking in from the outside.

6 Slowly and gradually resume regular breathing. Open your eyes, rise and return to your usual activities.

THE TREE

This pose will help you to achieve perfect balance and will strengthen and tone your back and legs.

NOTES AND SUGGESTIONS

• If you focus your attention on a still object in front of you, such as a door handle or a picture on a wall, it will help you to maintain your balance. You can also concentrate on your own rhythmic breathing.

1 Stand tall with your feet close together and parallel to each other. Establish good posture and breathe regularly.

2 Slowly lift one leg and, with the help of your hands, place the sole of the foot against the inner side of your opposite thigh, as high up as is comfortable. Bring your hands together in front of your breastbone. Alternatively, you may stretch your arms sideways at shoulder level, with your wrists relaxed (see right).

3 Stay in this posture for several seconds or as long as you comfortably can. Continue to breathe regularly.

4 When you are ready to come out of the posture, straighten your bent leg slowly and resume your starting position. Relax your hands at your sides.

5 Repeat the exercise, this time balancing on the other foot.

6 Rest briefly.

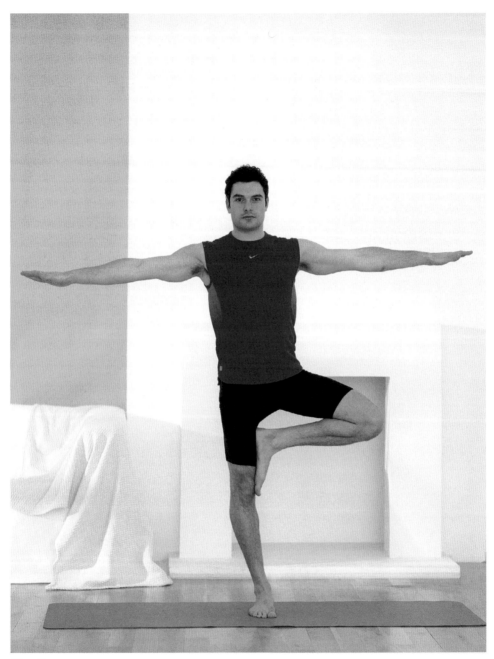

Step 2

BALANCE POSTURE

This posture enhances concentration and nerve-muscle coordination. Also called the quadriceps stretch, it conditions the quadriceps muscles at the front of the thighs, which help to straighten the knees.

NOTES AND SUGGESTIONS

• When doing this or any other balancing posture, fix your gaze on a still object, such as a door handle, a vase of flowers or a picture on a wall. It will help you to stay steady.

• Alternatively, focus your attention on your own slow, regular breathing.

1 Stand tall with your feet comfortably but not too far apart, and your body weight evenly distributed. Breathe regularly.

2 Shift your weight on to one foot. Focus your attention on your breathing to help you to stay steady, or on a still object in front of you, such as a door handle.

3 Bend your other leg and point the foot backward, grasp your foot with the hand on the same side, and bring it as close to the buttock on that side as you can with ease.

4 Raise your opposite arm straight up above you.

5 Maintain this posture for several seconds or as long as you wish, remembering to breathe regularly.

6 Slowly resume your starting position.

7 Repeat the exercise (steps 2 to 6) on the other side.

8 Rest.

Variation
When you have gained some mastery of this posture, you may welcome the challenge of a variation:

Slowly and carefully bend forward. At the same time, and still holding the foot of your bent leg, push it away from your buttocks. Move your body as a unit and keep breathing regularly.

Step 1

Step 4

Step 3

Step 7

SQUATTING

One quarter of the human race habitually take the weight off their feet by squatting. A deep squat position for work and rest is used by millions of people in Africa, Asia and Latin America.

WHAT IT DOES

Squatting reduces any exaggerated curve of the lower spine, thus lessening tension on spinal muscles and ligaments. It reduces pressure on spinal discs. Consequently, the back is both strengthened and relaxed, and back problems and discomfort are minimized. Squatting is also excellent for strengthening the ankles and feet.

NOTES AND SUGGESTIONS

- If you have varicose veins, alternately squat and get up again, several times in succession.

- Look for ways to incorporate squatting during daily activities: attending to a small child; dusting the lower parts of furniture; putting in or retrieving something from the lower drawer of a cabinet; weeding.

- I also like to practise squatting while waiting for the timer to signal that the evening meal is ready.

1 Stand with your legs comfortably apart. Distribute your body weight evenly between your feet. Breathe regularly.

2 Slowly bend your knees, lowering your buttocks until you are sitting on your heels. Bring your hands together as if in prayer (see right).

3 Stay in this posture for several seconds or as long as you comfortably can.

4 Resume your starting position.

CAUTION

- Avoid the squatting posture after the 34th week of pregnancy, until your baby's head is fully engaged, or if you experience pain in the pubic area. Avoid it if you have haemorrhoids or have had a cervical stitch inserted.

Step 2

MEDITATION

Think of meditation as a natural 'tool', rather than a mysterious, esoteric practice. It is a device used to relax the conscious mind without clouding awareness. Doctors describe the meditative state as one of 'hypometabolic wakefulness', which means that your metabolism has decreased even though you are still awake and conscious. They also refer to it as a state of 'restful alertness', an apparent contradiction.

WHAT HAPPENS?

When you are asleep, your heart rate becomes slower, oxygen consumption decreases and consciousness fades. When you are awake, by contrast, your heart rate quickens, oxygen consumption increases and you are usually alert. These opposites are united during meditation so that, although your body becomes deeply relaxed, you are conscious and your mind is clear.

Meditation, then, is a technique for quietening a restless mind and discouraging it from pursuing thoughts and ideas. You focus your attention on one thing or activity to the exclusion of everything else.

When the mind is quiet, you feel peaceful. With so many stimuli bombarding your senses every day and competing for our attention, it is no wonder that you might often feel stressed. Meditating regularly provides an antidote since it requires us, for a little while, to distance ourselves from these relentless environmental demands.

Meditation combats stress.

Meditate at a time when you know you will not be disturbed.

BENEFITS OF MEDITATION

Just as athletes tune and train their bodies, meditation tunes and trains the mind. For lasting value, it must be practised regularly. Regular meditation practice helps to bring deep-seated tensions to the surface so that you can examine them and attempt to resolve them.

BENEFITS OF MEDITATION

When you confront and deal honestly with unresolved personal issues, you begin to be more at ease with yourself and more comfortable in your relationships with others. This results in a greater sense of self-worth, more self-confidence and better productivity.

It also contributes to increased self-control, so that events and circumstances that previously seemed insurmountable now begin to appear manageable. Meditation helps to integrate and strengthen your personality, allowing you to become serene and competent.

Health implications

Long-term meditation also helps to decrease metabolic age. Studies show that people who meditate regularly visit their doctor and are admitted to hospital less frequently than those who do not meditate routinely. They also have a lower incidence of heart disease and cancer. Increasingly, doctors are recommending daily meditation as an adjunct to treatment for a variety of disorders including heart disease, high blood pressure, migraine,

You need to reach a state of restful alertness.

stomach and intestinal ulcers and certain nervous system conditions. Before starting to practise, however, you should always check with your doctor for advice on what you can and cannot achieve.

When to meditate

You can meditate before embarking on a long road journey, before a public appearance, in preparation for an interview or exam, before and after surgery, or before the children come home from school – any time, in fact, that you anticipate a demanding, or stressful situation.

HOW MEDITATION WORKS

During meditation, oxygen consumption and carbon dioxide elimination both decrease markedly without an alteration in their balance. This means that the circulatory system is functioning efficiently and that the heart's workload is reduced. The heart and respiration rates both decrease, indicating a state of deep relaxation.

Skin resistance increases significantly, denoting a calm emotional state. Metabolic rate drops by about 20 per cent, with a corresponding fall in blood pressure. Lactate ion concentration (thought to affect muscle tone and emotional state) decreases by about 33 per cent. And brainwave recordings on an electro-encephalograph (EEG)

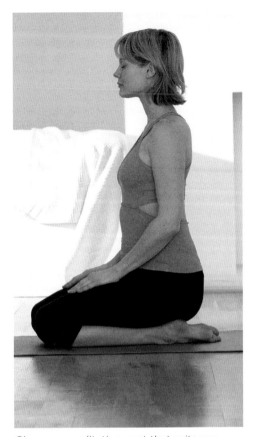

Choose a meditation post that suits you.

show an unusual abundance of alpha waves. These wave signify that the brain is alert yet also in a wonderfully relaxed state.

PREPARING TO MEDITATE

Because it is usually easier to gain control over the body than over the mind, a good way to start preparing for a session of meditation is to do the simple stretching exercises described in Chapter Two, or other similar exercises.

The next preparatory step for meditation is to be able to stay focused. All the exercises in this book will train you to do this, as they require attentiveness to the movements in synchronization with regular breathing. You will also find the balancing exercises such as the tree (see pp. 100–1) and the balance posture (see pp. 102–3) useful for this purpose.

In addition, doing the breathing exercises will promote the 'one-pointedness' that is necessary for successful meditation.

The right posture

Another prerequisite is the ability to sit still for up to 20 minutes at a time. Folded-leg postures such as the firm posture (see p. 115) and the easy pose (see pp. 116–17) will provide you with a stable base and enable you to hold your spine in good vertical alignment. If you find, however, that you are unable to sit for any length of time in one of these postures, choose a sitting position in which you are completely comfortable for the duration of the exercise and use a support for your spine if necessary.

Sitting still during meditation is important because the less movement and distraction there is, the steadier your mind will be.

Preparing for meditation

OTHER GUIDELINES

Meditation is both private and personal. You must find ways and times of meditating that suit you and your lifestyle. Here are some useful guidelines.

- Try to meditate at least once a day; preferably twice. Begin with five minutes per session and gradually increase it to 20 minutes, according to your circumstances and the time available.

- Daily practice of the pose of tranquillity (see pp. 132-7), or any convenient modification of the technique, will train you in the art of relaxing at will, and is therefore well worth your while.

- It's best to meditate before rather than after a meal so that the process of digestion doesn't interfere with your concentration.

- Choose a quiet place in which to meditate, where you can be assured of at least five minutes of uninterrupted time (to begin with), and about 20 minutes for a longer session.

- Suitable places include: a quiet room at home or at work; a small empty chapel; a private porch; a garden; beside a pond or lake.

- If after practising a particular meditation a few times you still do not feel comfortable with it, try another. There's no single way of meditating that is best for everyone.

- Through experimentation you will find the method that is most compatible with your personality and beliefs. You should always feel better, not worse, after a meditation session.

- Be patient and persevere in your meditation. Do not feel disappointed if the expected results are not immediately apparent. The benefits of regular meditation are cumulative, and skill and ease will come with time and repeated practice.

MEDITATION IN ACTION

Meditation is a focusing of attention on one thing or activity at a time, to the exclusion of everything else. You can apply this principle to many everyday tasks and so reap the benefits that regular meditation brings. These include: greater self-confidence, efficiency and productivity; better health in general and fewer visits to the doctor; slower ageing. When you are able to turn some of your activities into a meditation of sorts, you will find that you are less easily distracted and stressed.

SALAD MEDITATION

Here's an example of meditation in action, carried out by a friend of mine, as he prepared a tossed green salad for friends.

He seemed totally immersed in the process of meticulously cutting up onions and parsley from his kitchen garden; carefully washing and drying green lettuce leaves and breaking them into bite-sized pieces; slicing and dicing red, ripe tomatoes and radishes and attentively combining all the ingredients before the final tossing with olive oil and vinegar.

He remarked that this was his meditation, so absorbed was he in this activity, and added that when he was engaged in making a salad, he was able to shut everything else out of his mind and so found it a very therapeutic exercise.

Think of the many things you do in the course of the day. Think of which ones you can realistically do with a similar one-pointedness: arranging flowers; listening as a child or other friend speaks; playing tennis. Put this idea of meditation in action into practice and you will be pleasantly surprised at the results.

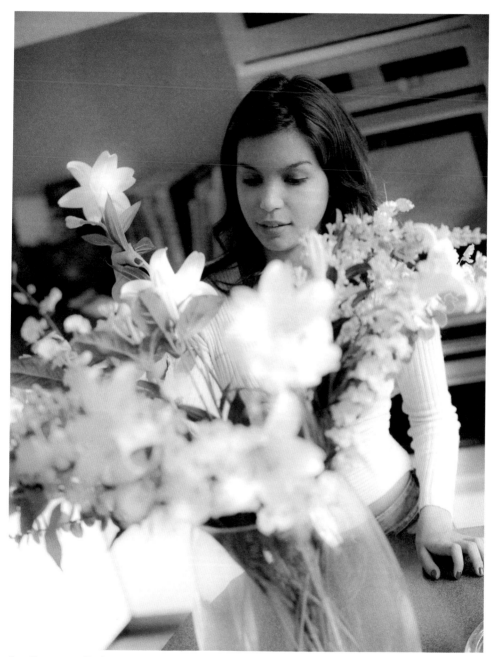

See if you can find your own methods of meditation in action.

A SIMPLE MEDITATION

Meditation is a natural device for relaxing your conscious mind without dulling your awareness. It helps to keep you in the present, as an antidote to apprehension, worry and depression, which concern past and future events.

NOTES AND SUGGESTIONS

You may substitute any word or short phrase for the word 'one' in the exercise on the right. Particularly effective is something related to your religion or other belief system. Suggestions are: 'peace' and 'calm'.

• When faced with a challenge, try to recall the calm you experienced during or after meditation. Take a few slow breaths, as deep as you can without straining. These simple measures will help to delay your response, so that you will act consciously rather than impulsively.

• Keep your breathing slow and smooth throughout.

• If your thoughts wander during your meditation, gently guide them back to both the breathing and the repetition of your chosen phrase. With practice, your thoughts will drift off less often as your ability to remain focused improves. Be patient and persevere.

1 Sit comfortably upright, with the crown of your head uppermost. Relax your whole body. Close your eyes and inhale slowly and smoothly through your nose.

2 As you exhale slowly and smoothly through your nose, mentally say the word 'one'.

3 Repeat steps 1 and 2 several times in smooth succession.

4 When you are ready to end your period of meditation, do so slowly: open your eyes and gently stretch or massage your limbs.

Step 1

FIRM POSTURE

This posture encourages good spinal alignment and therefore healthier functioning of vital structures within the trunk. It is also a useful meditation posture, providing a solid, stable base on which to sit.

NOTES AND SUGGESTIONS

- If at first your heels cannot bear your weight on them, place a cushion between your buttocks and your heels, and stay in this position only briefly.

- As your knees and ankles become more flexible and your body more conditioned, you will be able to maintain the firm posture for a longer time.

Step 2

1 Kneel down with your legs together and your body erect but not rigid. Let your feet point straight backward.

2 Slowly lower your body to sit on your heels. Gently place your palms on your knees.

3 Sit tall and breathe regularly. Keep as relaxed as you can.

EASY POSE

The easy pose (tailor sitting) provides a stable base and encourages you to hold your spine naturally erect. It promotes relaxation of the back muscles. It brings into play the sartorius, or tailor muscles, which lie across the thighs, from about the front of the hip bones to the shin bones. These are the muscles used in bending the legs and turning them inward.

NOTES AND SUGGESTIONS

• You may find it helpful to sit on a cushion or a folded towel or blanket, so that your knees come closer to the floor than they otherwise would.

• Because of the firm, stable base this posture provides, it is an excellent one in which to sit for a long period of time, as when meditating or doing breathing exercises.

• In addition, because easy pose encourages good spinal alignment, it is superb for promoting good posture and related feelings of self-worth and self-confidence.

1 Sit with your legs stretched out in front of you and your hands flat on the floor beside your hips.

2 Bend one leg at the knee and place the foot of that leg under the opposite thigh.

3 Bend the other leg and place the foot under the opposite bent leg.

4 Rest your palms gently on your knees or place them upturned, one in the other, in your lap.

5 Maintain this posture as long as you comfortably can, breathing regularly and keeping your body fully relaxed.

Step 1

Step 3

Step 2

Step 4

CAUTION

- Avoid sitting in this or any other folded-legs posture if you experience pain in your pubic area.

YOGA FOR BEDTIME

Sleep experts say that many people who live in industrialized countries are sleep deprived. This is not surprising. Youngsters, for example, get up earlier than they normally would to accommodate the expanding size of many classes at school. They then rush to part-time jobs after their day's studies. In addition, there's homework to do, and sometimes cramming for a test the next day.

There are also extra-curricular activities such as soccer, hockey, or track and field practice. All this means going to bed late and being rudely awakened, after perhaps only six hours sleep, by the unwelcome ringing of an alarm clock.

Getting a good night's sleep makes all the difference to how you feel, so it's worth spending a little time preparing for bedtime to ensure that you get the best sleep possible.

THE ROLE OF SLEEP

Sleep fulfils two important functions: the restoration of energy and the regulation and resynchronization of the body. Sleep deprivation over time can have serious consequences, among which are low energy and motivation, poor concentration and performance and, in more extreme cases, depression and psychosis.

Promoting quality sleep

If lack of sleep has resulted in ill health, please consult a doctor. There are several simple measures you can take to help prevent this, and to promote sound, refreshing sleep. If you cannot immediately add to the number of hours of sleep you are currently obtaining, you can certainly do something about the quality of your sleep.

Mild exercise after supper can promote sleep of good quality, whereas more vigorous activity may prove too stimulating. Most of the warm-up exercises in Chapter Two are suitable for evening practice. The breathing exercises (except for the dynamic cleansing breath) are also appropriate. A warm (not hot) bath, in which the water is between 35°C and 38°C (95°F and 100°F) is relaxing, and some people find it sleep-inducing. The addition of an aromatic oil with calming properties,

Preparing for sleep

such as bergamot, cedarwood, chamomile, lavender, neroli, or rose, may enhance the mellow mood conducive to sweet sleep.

Calming measures

Just before going to bed, avoid reading material that is highly stimulating or watching television shows which are disturbing or exciting, if you have observed that they prevent you from sleeping soundly in the past.

As you prepare yourself for sleep, turn your thoughts away from unpleasant matters. If possible, try to resolve any misunderstandings or other discord before you finally turn in for the night. Practise the pose of tranquillity (see pp. 132–7) or the alternate nostril breathing (see pp. 138–9).

Should you experience difficulty falling or staying asleep because of hunger, try eating a light carbohydrate snack before you go to bed.

Consider also taking two or three calcium tablets with warm milk, but first check with your doctor or a qualified nutrition counsellor.

Avoid drinking alcohol or smoking shortly before going to sleep. Alcohol may help you fall asleep, but it will also cause you to have a restless night, leaving you feeling groggy and tired when you wake up. Avoid stimulants such as regular tea, coffee, cocoa and cola drinks. There are many relaxing herbal teas that are more suitable for drinking at bedtime. Check with your doctor to ensure that the herbal infusion of your choice will not clash with any medication you take.

Maximum comfort

Make sure that the room in which you habitually sleep is sufficiently warm or cool, dark or softly lit, as you prefer and free of any disturbing sights or sounds.

Sleep on a mattress that adequately supports your back without being rigid, keep the bedclothes to the minimum necessary for desired warmth or coolness, use a pillow that gives your head and neck good support and wear loose, comfortable clothing.

Herbal aids

To aid a good night's sleep drink a herbal tea made with catmint, chamomile flowers, dill, lime blossom, passion flowers or valerian, all of which induce a pleasant drowsiness. However, please check with your doctor that the herbal tea of your choice will not react with any medication you are taking.

Chamomile tea is one of several calming herbal infusions.

TEN-MINUTE EVENING SEQUENCE

The ten-minute pre-sleep exercise sequence that follows on the following pages is designed to counteract any tension that you may have accumulated during the day, to promote relaxation and to set a scene conducive to peaceful sleep. Modify the sequence to suit your own special needs. You can do so by reducing or increasing the number of repetitions, for example, or by increasing or decreasing the 'holding' period during which you maintain a particular stretch or posture.

1 Start the sequence by performing a number of neck stretches (see pp. 28–9) – 3 to 5 times in each direction.

Neck stretch, left

Neck stretch, right

Neck stretch, backward

Neck stretch, forward

2 Progress to several shoulder exercises (shrugs or rotations, see pp. 32–3) – again, 3 to 5 times each.

3 Move on to ankle rotations, (see p. 42) repeating 3 to 5 times in each direction.

Shoulder rotation

4 Perform the pelvic tilt on all fours
  (see p. 126) 3 to 5 times.

Pelvic tilt, step 1

Pelvic tilt, step 2

5 Afterward, rest in the curling leaf
  posture (see p. 127).

Curling leaf, step 2

6 Then work through the half or full shoulderstand (see pp. 128–9 and 130–1). Maintain the posture for 20 to 60 seconds or more. Alternatively, you can do the legs-up posture (see p. 98).

7 For recovery do the pose of tranquillity (see pp. 132–7) or alternate nostril breathing (see pp. 138–39) for the time remaining, or lie in the legs-up posture (see p. 98) and practise all-body breathing (see p. 99), or indeed any other breathing exercise of your choice (except the dynamic cleansing breath).

All-body breathing

Pose of tranquillity, step 2

Legs up, step 1

PELVIC TILT ON ALL FOURS

Pelvic tilting helps to keep your spine flexible. It conditions the back muscles, which support your spine and tones and firms your abdominal muscles, which complement your back muscles as spinal supports.

1 Get on your hands and knees in the all fours position.

2 Exhaling, lower your head, tuck your hips down and arch your shoulders, so that your entire back is rounded. Concentrate on the tilting of the pelvis rather than on the arching of the shoulders.

3 Inhale and resume your starting position (step 1).

4 Repeat steps 2 and 3 several times in smooth succession.

5 Rest.

Step 1

Step 2

CURLING LEAF

This posture, which is also called the pose of a child, helps to keep your spine flexible. As you breathe regularly while maintaining the completed posture, your internal organs receive a gentle, therapeutic massage, which promotes circulation and facilitates elimination. Curling leaf is also a very relaxing posture and an excellent one to practise following backward-bending exercises.

NOTES AND SUGGESTIONS

Step 2

- If you cannot get your head down on to the mat, place a cushion, pillow, or folded towel in front of you and rest your forehead on it.

1 Sit on your heels, as in the firm posture. Relax your jaw and breathe regularly.

2 Bend forward slowly, and rest your forehead on the mat; or turn your face to the side. Relax your arms and hands beside you. Stay in this posture for several seconds or for as long as you feel comfortable in it, breathing regularly.

3 Slowly resume your starting position.

Step 3

HALF SHOULDERSTAND

The health-giving benefits of this inverted posture are the result of the stretching and contraction of three muscle groups: your back muscles which are stretched, your abdominal muscles which are contracted and the muscles at the front of your neck which are also contracted.

The organs within your torso are revitalized, thereby improving circulation and also the function of the endocrine glands and the nervous system. By summoning the aid of gravitational forces, moreover, the half shoulderstand (and other inverted postures) promotes circulation to the upper body, including the face and scalp, and so enriches those tissues.

1 Lie on your back. Bend your knees and rest the soles of your feet flat on the mat. Keep your arms close to your sides. Breathe regularly throughout the exercise.

2 Bring first one knee, then the other, to your chest.

3 Straighten one leg at a time until your feet are pointing upward.

4 Kick backward with both feet at once, until your hips are off the mat. Support your hips with your hands, thumbs in front.

5 Maintain this posture for a few seconds to begin with; longer as you become more comfortable with it.

6 To come out of the posture, rest your hands on the mat, close to your body. Keep your head firmly pressed to the mat (perhaps tilting your chin slightly upward), and slowly and carefully lower your torso, from top to bottom, on to the mat. Bend your knees and stretch out your legs – first one, and then the other.

7 Rest.

Step 1

Step 2

Step 4

Step 6

CAUTIONS

- Avoid this and other inverted postures if you have an eye or ear disorder, or if you suffer from heart disease, high blood pressure or other circulatory abnormality.

- Do not practise inverted postures while you are menstruating.

- Check with your doctor before attempting to do the half shoulderstand or other head-low, hips-high postures.

FULL SHOULDERSTAND

The benefits derived from the full shoulderstand are the same as those of the half shoulderstand (see pp. 128–9). In addition, the full shoulderstand enhances thyroid gland function: the thyroid gland controls your body's metabolism, so that when it is functioning well all cells and tissues benefit.

1 Lie on your back. Bend your knees and rest the soles of your feet flat on the mat. Keep your arms close to your sides. Breathe regularly throughout the exercise.

2 Bring first one knee, then the other, to your chest.

3 Straighten one leg at a time until your feet are pointing upward.

4 Kick back with both feet at once, until your hips are off the mat. Support your hips with your hands, with your thumbs in front.

5 Gradually move your hands, one at a time, toward your upper back, until your body is in as vertical a position as you can manage with complete comfort. Your chin should then come in contact with your chest, and your whole body should be as relaxed as possible.

6 Maintain this posture for a few seconds to begin with, working up to a minute or more as you become more comfortable with it.

7 To come out of the posture, tilt your feet slightly backward. Rest your arms beside your body and keep your head pressed to the mat. Slowly lower your hips to the mat. Bend your legs at the knees and lower them slowly, one at a time, on to the mat.

8 Rest.

Step 3

Step 5

POSE OF TRANQUILLITY

This is a splendid exercise for helping to combat many forms of stress. Practised in the evening after a day of intense work, it is excellent for inducing sound, refreshing sleep. It is also very useful in the management of pain and anxiety states, and for counteracting fatigue and promoting calm. Regular practice of the technique also helps to keep blood pressure within the normal range, and it is, in addition, a beneficial complement to treatments for heart disorders and peptic ulcers.

NOTES AND SUGGESTIONS

• You may practise the pose of tranquillity in bed, if you are unwell, for instance; or in a reclining chair that gives adequate support to your neck and back.

• Modify the exercise instructions accordingly. You may also practise it while lying on your back, with your knees bent and your lower legs resting on a padded chair. Or you may practise it in the legs-up posture (see p. 98).

• Use whatever props and aids you need to provide good support for your body, particularly your neck and lower back, so that you are very comfortable. Suitable props include rolled or folded towels, folded blankets, pillows, or cushions.

• Keep a sweater or blanket and a pair of warm socks nearby. Use them to prevent you becoming cold as your body cools down during relaxation.

• Loosely tie a scarf around your eyes, or wear a pair of eye-shades to hasten relaxation by the complete exclusion of light.

• In step 13 of the exercise instructions, use imagery with which you feel most comfortable. You may, for example, visualize yourself lying on a warm, sandy beach while a gentle breeze caresses your face, arms and legs. Each time you breathe in, imagine the surf rolling toward your feet, bringing peace and rejuvenating properties with it. Each time you breathe out, imagine the surf rolling out again, taking with it the cares, concerns and weariness of the day.

- Practise the pose of tranquillity any time you need to recharge and re-energize yourself, such as after an especially demanding day or a particularly trying experience that has left you feeling drained. • Practise it when you feel anxiety mounting and when you long for a sense of calm and well-being.

- Do this relaxation technique in a quiet place where you can be sure of 10 to 20 minutes on your own without interruption.

When you are well versed in the technique, you can dispense with alternately tightening and relaxing muscle groups and so reduce the time required to practise it. For example, while focusing attention on your feet, mentally say: 'Feet, let go of your tightness. Relax.' Then consciously relax them. Work from the feet right up to the facial muscles.

Record your voice

If it makes it easier for you, you can record the instructions for the pose of tranquillity using a tape-recorder. Speak slowly and soothingly, or ask a friend with a clear, pleasing voice to do so for you. Listen to the recording as the need arises.

1 Lie on your back with your legs comfortably separated and stretched out in front of you. Relax your arms at your sides, a little away from your body, with your palms upturned. Position your head for maximum comfort and close your eyes. Relax your jaw and breathe regularly. This is the basic position. Suggestions for variations are given in the notes and suggestions.

2 Push your heels away, bringing your toes toward you. Note the resulting stiffness in your legs.

This entire exercise is performed lying on your back.

Maintain this tension for a few seconds, but continue to breathe regularly. (This maintaining of tension will be referred to as 'hold' from now on.)

3 Let go of the stiffness. Relax your knees, legs, ankles, feet and toes. (This letting go of tension will be referred to as 'release' from now on.) Let your legs sink with their full weight on to the mat.

Step 2

4 Tighten your buttocks. Hold. Release. Relax your hips. On exhalation, press the small of your back (waist) firmly toward the mat. Feel your abdominal muscles tighten. Hold the tightness as long as your exhalation lasts. Release the tension as you inhale. Breathe regularly. Relax your back and abdomen. (This is a lying version of the pelvic tilt earlier in this book (pp.xx–xx).

5 Inhale and squeeze your shoulder blades together. Release as you exhale. Relax your shoulders and upper back. Breathe regularly.

6 Shrug your shoulders as if trying to touch your ears with them. Relax your shoulders on release.

Step 6

7 Carefully tilt your head slightly backward. Feel the gentle stretch of your neck. Carefully re-position your head for maximum comfort. Relax your throat.

8 Carefully tilt your head forward as far as is comfortable, tucking in your chin. Hold. Release to neutral position. Relax your neck for a short time.

Step 7

Step 8

9 Raise your eyebrows and wrinkle your forehead. Hold. Release. Relax your forehead. Relax your scalp muscle, which goes from just above the eyebrows to the back of the head.

Step 9

10 Squeeze your eyes shut tightly. Hold. Release. Relax your eyes.

11 Exhaling, open your mouth wide. Stick out your tongue as far as you comfortably can. Open your eyes wide, as if staring. Feel all your facial muscles tighten. (This is the lion pose, which can be done as a separate exercise to reduce facial tension.) Hold the tension as long as your exhalation lasts. Inhale and pull in your tongue. Close your mouth and eyes. Relax your jaw, tongue, lips, throat and facial muscles. Breathe regularly.

Step 11

12 Stiffen and raise your arms. Make tight fists. Hold. Release. Relax your arms and hands. Let them sink heavily on to the mat.

13 Now give your full attention to your breathing. As you inhale slowly and as deeply as you can without strain, visualize filling your system not only with health-giving oxygen, but also with positive forces such as love, hope, joy and calm. As you exhale smoothly without force, visualize eliminating from your body not only wastes such as carbon dioxide, but also negative influences such as sadness, resentment, anxiety and hopelessness. Each time you exhale, let your body sink a little more into the mat, until every trace of residual tension has vanished.

14 When you feel ready to end your session of deep relaxation, do so slowly and with awareness: make small, gentle movements, such as wriggling your toes and fingers, or rolling your head from side to side. You may also, if you wish, gently massage parts of your body. When ready to sit up, roll on to your side and use your hands to help you. Do not come straight up from a supine position, as this may put a strain your back. Never get up suddenly.

Step 12

NOSTRIL BREATHING

This exercise stimulates the inner lining of the nose by altering the air flow and sending sequential impulses to the two hemispheres of the brain. Alternate nostril breathing helps to integrate the functioning of these two hemispheres. The results include a harmonizing of mind and body, and greater mental and physical energy when this is needed.

This is a very soothing exercise that helps to counteract anxiety, which can aggravate pain and other discomforts. It is, in addition, a useful antidote for sleeplessness.

NOTES AND SUGGESTIONS

• You may try alternate nostril breathing while standing, or even while lying down.

• With your eyes open, you can try this exercise (and most of the other breathing exercises in this book) in a variety of places, including your child's school, your bedside, at your desk or computer, filing cabinet, photocopier or fax machine (if you can do so unobserved), while waiting to pick up a child from a party, in a parked car and during television advertising breaks. Look out for opportunities that work for you and modify the exercises to suit yourself.

1 Sit or stand tall and observe good posture. Relax your body, relax your jaw and breathe regularly.

2 Rest your left hand in your lap, on your thigh or knee, or on the arm rest of a chair.

3 Arrange the fingers of your right hand as follows: fold the two middle fingers toward your palm (or rest them lightly on the bridge of your nose). Use your thumb on your right nostril, once the exercise is in progress, and your ring finger (or ring and little fingers) on your left nostril.

4 Close your eyes and begin. Close your right nostril and inhale slowly, smoothly, and as deeply as you can without strain, through your left nostril.

5 Close your left nostril and release the closure of your right nostril. Exhale gently.

Step 3

Step 4

6 Inhale slowly and deeply through your right nostril.

7 Close your right nostril and release the closure of your left nostril. Exhale.

This completes one 'round' of alternate nostril breathing.

8 Repeat steps 4 to 7 in smooth succession as many times as you wish, until you begin to feel a sense of calm.

9 Relax your right arm and hand. Resume regular breathing. Open your eyes.

WEEKEND YOGA PROGRAMME

The yoga exercises that you have been incorporating into your daily schedule throughout the week will have trained and conditioned your body and mind in a slow and gentle way, in readiness for a longer weekend workout. Here is a sample programme, which you can modify to suit your own unique requirements. It lasts from 30 minutes to one hour.

ABOUT THE PROGRAMME

The postures and other exercises in this specimen workout have been carefully selected to: warm up your body; provide arm and leg stretches; exercise your spine backward, forward and sideways, and also give it gentle torsion (twisting); tone and firm the four sets of abdominal muscles that form what is known as the 'abdominal corset', and which contribute to spinal health.

The programme includes, in addition, an inverted posture to help counteract the effects of the constant downward pull of gravity, and breathing, concentration, visualization, meditation and relaxation techniques to assist you in regaining a sense of calm and control.

The exercises that follow are arranged so as to allow for a smooth transition from one to the other, but you can vary their order as you wish.

1 Start the sequence by performing a number of neck stretches (see pp. 28–9) – 3 to 5 times in each direction.

2 Now perfrom the butterfly (see pp. 38–9) 15 to 30 times.

3 Move on to the lying twist (see pp. 36–7), working 5 to 8 times in each direction.

4 Continue with the Sun salutations (see pp. 43–7). Performing 2 to 6 sets in all.

Neck stretch

Butterfly

Lying twist

Sun salutations

5 Now perform the half moon pose (see p. 142).

Half moon

6 Follow the half moon pose with the tree pose (see pp. 100–1) or balance posture (see pp. 102–3).

The tree

7 Sit on your mat and work through the spinal twist (see pp. 150–1).

8 Progress from the spinal twist to the yoga sit-up (see p. 152).

9 From the yoga sit-up, move on to the pelvic tilt on all fours (see p. 126).

10 Follow the pelvic tilt with the bridge (see pp. 148–9).

11 Now work through the half or full shoulderstand (see pp. 128–9 or 130–1).

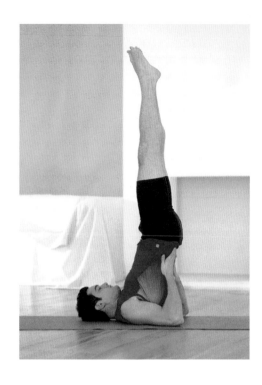

12 As you begin to reach the end of the programme, perform a breathing exercise of your choice.

13 Progress to the humming breath (see p. 153) or other meditation of your choice.

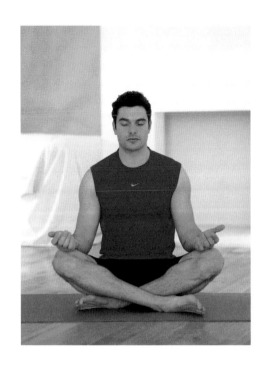

14 Complete the programme with step 1 of the pose of tranquillity (see pp. 132–7).

THE HALF MOON

The half moon gives a lateral (sideways) stretch to your torso, and so contributes to the health of your spine. It also helps to keep your shoulder joints flexible and it exercises the midriff to discourage a build-up of fat. In addition, it facilitates deep breathing.

NOTES AND SUGGESTIONS

• In step 2, keep your arms alongside your ears, so that when you bend it will be a true sideways bend rather than a forward bend.

1 Stand naturally erect, with your feet close together and your body weight evenly distributed between them. Relax your jaw and breathe regularly.

2 On an inhalation, bring your arms upward, pressing your palms together if you can.

3 As you exhale, slowly and carefully bend your body to one side to form a graceful sideways arch.

4 Hold the posture for several seconds or as long as you comfortably can while breathing regularly.

5 Inhale and bring your arms back to the upright position. Exhale and lower your arms to your sides.

6 Repeat the exercise on the other side.

7 Rest.

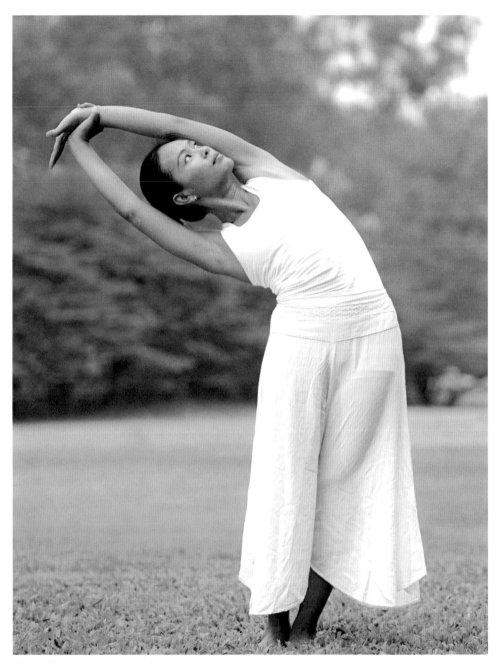

The half moon pose, step 4

THE BRIDGE

Excellent for toning the back and abdominal muscles, the bridge also helps to keep your spine strong and flexible, and gives your body a therapeutic stretch.

NOTES AND SUGGESTIONS

• Combine with the lying pelvic tilt (p. xx). Do the pelvic tilt first, then move smoothly into the bridge.

• Or try this variation: fully stretch your arms and fingers overhead and point your knees as far from your body as you comfortably can.

1 Lie on your back with your legs bent and the soles of your feet flat on the mat, comfortably close to your buttocks. Relax your arms close to your sides, with your palms turned downward. Relax your jaw and breathe regularly.

2 Inhaling, raise your hips, then slowly and smoothly raise the rest of your back until your torso is fully raised. Remember to keep your arms and hands pressed to the mat.

3 Hold the posture for as long as you are comfortable in it, while continuing to breathe regularly.

4 Slowly and smoothly lower your torso in reverse motion, from top to bottom, as if curling your spine one bone at a time on to the mat. Synchronize regular breathing with this movement. Stretch out your legs, turn your palms upward and rest.

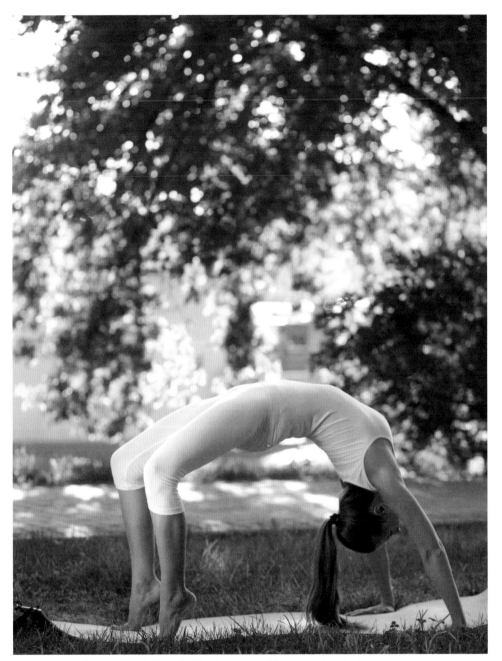

An advanced form of the bridge holds the pose with arms extended.

SPINAL TWIST

This is the only yoga posture that requires maximum torsion (twisting) of the spine, first to one side then to the other, causing the vertebrae to rotate one over the other and, at the same time, to bend to the right or left. This spinal action gives a therapeutic massage to nerves branching off the spinal column. The muscles of the lower back are also stretched and contracted during the exercise. This enhances the blood circulation in the area of your kidneys and revitalizes your adrenal glands (located on top of the kidneys).

1 Sit naturally erect on the mat, with your legs stretched out in front of you. Relax your jaw and breathe regularly.

2 Bend your left leg at the knee and place your left foot beside the outer side of your right knee.

3 Exhaling, slowly and smoothly twist your body to the left and rest both hands on the mat on your left side. Turn your head to look over your left shoulder.

Step 1

Step 2

4 Hold the posture for several seconds or as long as you can with absolute comfort. Keep breathing regularly.

5 Slowly untwist and return to your starting position.

6 Rest briefly.

Repeat the twist on the right side, as follows:

7 Stretch out your left leg in front of you.

8 Bend your right leg at the knee and place your right foot beside the outer side of your left knee.

9 As you exhale, slowly and carefully twist your body to the right and place both hands on the mat at your right side. Turn your head and look over your right shoulder.

10 Hold the posture for several seconds or as long as you can with absolute comfort. Continue to breathe regularly.

11 Slowly untwist and return to your starting position.

12 Rest.

Step 4

Step 10

YOGA SIT-UP

Safer to do than the conventional sit-up, the yoga sit-up is superb for developing and maintaining the strength of the abdominal muscles. Strong abdominal muscles help to support the back muscles, and so contribute to the health of the spine.

1 Lie on your back with your legs stretched out in front of you and slightly separated. Relax your arms at your sides. Relax your jaw and breathe regularly.

2 Bend your knees and slide your feet toward your buttocks until the soles are flat on the mat. (Maintain this distance between the feet and buttocks as you practise the sit-up.) Rest your palms on your thighs.

3 Exhale as you slowly and carefully raise your head. Keep your gaze on your hands as you slide them along your thighs, as if to touch your knees.

4 When you have reached the maximum tolerable tension in your abdomen, stop and hold the posture for a few seconds, or as long as you comfortably can. Keep breathing regularly.

5 Inhale and resume your starting position by slowly curling your spine back on to the mat. Relax your arms and hands at your sides and rest.

Step 2

Step 3

HUMMING BREATH

Sounds can have a powerful effect on the mind. Military music on the battlefield or chants by cheerleaders, for example, tend to excite or agitate people or make them feel aggressive. Other sounds, such as those of a waterfall or a lullaby can promote relaxation and a sense of tranquillity.

One time-honoured way of focusing the mind is to meditate on the repetition of a selected sound. Choose one with which you are comfortable, and which is compatible with your belief system.

The most basic sound is that produced by humming. According to meditation tradition, all sounds are derived from this. It is a very peaceful sound. Interestingly, it is found, with variations, in almost every culture and religious tradition, as part of prayer or meditative ritual. In some instances, the words containing this sound mean 'peace' when translated literally: for example 'shalom' in Hebrew and 'salaam' in Arabic.

NOTES AND SUGGESTIONS

• Practise the humming breath after a busy or demanding day to help you to regain perspective and a feeling of self-control. Practise it when you feel troubled, to relax and comfort you. Give your complete attention to the breathing and the sound. This pulls your thoughts away from disturbing stimuli.

1 Sit upright with the crown of your head uppermost. Relax your hands. Close your eyes. Relax your jaw and breathe regularly through your nose.

2 Inhale slowly, smoothly and as deeply as you can without strain.

3 As you exhale slowly and smoothly, make a humming sound, like that of a bee. Let the humming last as long as your exhalation does.

4 Repeat steps 2 and 3 in smooth succession, as many times as you wish, until you feel calm and fully relaxed.

5 Resume regular breathing. Open your eyes as you draw the exercise to a close.

'Yoga is a light, which once lit, will never dim. The better your practice, the brighter the flame.'

B K S Iyengar

FURTHER READING

Benson, Herbert
The Relaxation Response
William Morrow, 1975

Feuerstein, Georg, Ph.D.
The Yoga Tradition
Hohm Press, 1998

Haynes, Marion E.
Personal Time Management (3rd ed.)
Crisp Learning, 2001

LeShan, Lawrence
How to Meditate
Turnstone Press, 1983

Monro, Dr Robin, Nagarathna, Dr R.,
and Nagendra, Dr H.R.
Yoga for Common Ailments
Gaia Books, 1990

Moyers, Bill
Healing and the Mind
Doubleday, 1993

Rama, Swami, Ballentine, Rudolph,
M.D., and Hymes, Alan, M.D.
Science of Breath
The Himalayan International Institute
of Yoga Science and Philosophy, 1979

Stroebel, Charles F., M.D.
QR The Quieting Reflex
G.Putnam's Sons, 1982

Weil, Andrew, M.D.
Ask Dr. Weil
The Ballantine Publishing Group, 1998

Weil, Andrew, M.D.
Spontaneous Healing
Alfred A. Knopf, 1995

Weller, Stella
Good Housekeeping Complete Yoga
HarperCollins Illustrated, 2001

Weller, Stella
The Yoga Back Book (rev. ed.)
Thorsons, 2000

Weller, Stella
Well Being for Women
Godsfield Press and Sterling, 1999

Weller, Stella
Yoga Therapy
Thorsons, 1995

INDEX

ACKNOWLEDGEMENTS

Author's dedication

To Gundel, with much love and gratitude

Author's acknowledgements

Many thanks to everyone who has contributed to this book. I am particularly grateful to Joss Pearson, Gerardine Munroe, Patrick Nugent, Pip Morgan and the editorial and sales staff at Gaia Books. Thanks also to Michael Whitehead and Warrick Sears of Bridgewater Books, Fiona Biggs, Mike Hemsley, Adam Clement and Rebecca Barkans.

Special thanks go to David for sharing his expertise in computer skills, and to Walter and Karl for their unfailing support.

CAUTIONS

Care is needed when treating the very young, the elderly, and those suffering from bone problems, epilepsy, clinical depression, cancer, low or high blood pressure, or who are pregnant.

PERSONAL DETAILS

Stella Weller is a master of Hatha Yoga and a published author for more than 20 years, specialising in yoga and other health-related subjects. She has more than 12 books in print, some translated into as many as ten languages.

Stella lives in Vancouver, Canada, where she has worked as a Registered Nurse for more than fifteen years. She teaches people how to integrate yoga into their lives, especially those suffering from anxiety and other stress-related disorders.

PICTURE CREDITS

Dreamstime.com Artofphoto 107; Diego Vito Cervo 91; Dmitry Bairachnyi 149; Dmitry Kalinovsky 15; Goodluz 75; Hongqi Zhang (aka Michael Zhang) 10; Laindiapiaroa 17; Mallivan 49; Marina Pissarova 22, 50, 70, 92, 154; Monkey Business Images 55; Nyul 97; Paul Prescott 65; Phil Date 113; Sashahaltam 7; Sidelnikov 19; Stefano Lunardi 77; Syda Productions 18; Szefei 20; Tinnakorn Srivichai 147; Valentyn75 76; Wavebreakmedia Ltd. 11, 27, 85, 87, 88.

Additional photography by Ruth Jenkinson for Octopus Publishing; royalty free